SCOTLAND 100 YEARS AGO
The charm of old Scotland illustrated

FLOWERDALE, GAIRLOCH, ROSS-SHIRE.

SCOTLAND
100 YEARS AGO
The charm of old Scotland illustrated

by

Samuel G. Green, D.D.

AFTON WATER.

Bracken Books
LONDON

First published 1886
by The Religious Tract Society.

This edition published by Bracken Books
a division of Bestseller Publications Limited,
Brent House, 24 Friern Park, North Finchley,
London N12 9DA
and copyright © Bracken Books 1985.

ISBN 0 946495 47 5

Printed and bound by R. J. Acford,
Chichester, England.

CARRON SIDE.

PREFACE.

A FRIEND who has read these pages while passing through the press has
suggested that the brighter side of a visit to Scotland is too exclusively
given—that more stress ought to have been laid on the probabilities of bad
weather, and the miseries of a "Scotch mist"; that a word of warning
might not have been misplaced as to the dearness of Highland hotels, and
the high rates charged for posting; and that English readers might have
been put on their guard as to the uncompromising temper and blunt address
of some with whom they would have to do. Well, all these points have to
be considered; and yet with every drawback, the delight remains. Even
broken weather has its intervals, the brighter and more exhilarating for the
storm or mist that has preceded; while no lover of the sublime and beautiful
would willingly exchange the grandeurs and terrors of the mountain gloom,
even for days of unclouded sunshine. But, as a matter of fact, I can
attest from the experience of many a tour, the weather is seldom or never
so bad for long together as absolutely to prevent, or even greatly to injure
enjoyment. Then as to the other criticisms: it must be admitted that, unless
a traveller is very wary and thrifty, he will not find a tour in Scotland the
most economical form of enjoyment. Something is to be said in excuse for
high charges, when the season is necessarily so short; yet I confess I have
found things much the same out of the season, when there has been no
competitive rush of tourists. There is room for improvement in some places
that might be mentioned; and it is satisfactory to learn, on the high
authority of Mr. J. B. Baddeley,[*] that the Scottish hotel system is decidedly

* *The Northern Highlands and Islands* ("Thorough Guide" Series). London, 1883. p. xiii.

improving, in this and other respects. For those who do not care to travel from place to place, the great Hydropathic establishments in almost every popular resort afford attractions hardly anywhere to be surpassed.

It is no part of our business to institute comparisons between Scotland and other countries, in their attraction for tourists. We can but say that it is something to be able to travel where there is no sea to cross, no Custom House to annoy, no foreign tongue with whose difficulties to grapple, no distraction to interfere with the calm enjoyment of the Lord's Day; where there is enough of difference from ordinary English life to give the charm of novelty, with enough of resemblance to show that we are still at home. The climate, too, in every bracing quality must be declared unsurpassed, even in the Alps; and there can hardly be a fresher, fuller glow of health than that which is imparted by a stay at Strathpeffer or Castleton in Braemar; while such marine resorts as Rothesay, Whiting Bay, Nairn, and many others, combine with these invigorating elements all the charms of the seaside for those who welcome its purer enjoyments apart from the intrusion of a noisy crowd. Of the delights of the Western Coast, with its sea lochs, cliffs and islands, to all who love the sea, and can enjoy a cruise, even when the waters are stormy, enough, but not too much, has been said in the following pages. Mr. William Black has portrayed for multitudes of readers the glories of yachting excursions amid these scenes; and even to the many, who must confine themselves to the steamers which leave the Clyde for these coasts continually all the summer through, there is hardly a form of enjoyment more exquisite or more health giving. In this respect at least, a Scottish excursion surpasses any other attainable in these latitudes.

The following pages contain memorials of several tours in Scotland, undertaken at different periods of the year; and it may honestly be certified that some of the most delightful of these were made "out of the season." In spring, the snow lingers on the mountain summits long after the valleys are bright with verdure and with flowers, and many a prospect in April and May is Alpine in its variety and splendour. June is generally a month of surpassing beauty in the Highlands; but there are few, save a few fishers, to behold the loveliness. We English people have mostly to defer our holidays until the year has past its prime, and, save for the blossoming heather, the charms of wood and moor and mountain glen are already beginning to wane. The "swift steamers" and coaches, indeed, are in many cases not placed upon their several routes until the middle of July, and the railway trains are mostly slow.

These public conveyances, while, of course the most economical, are also generally the most enjoyable means of effecting a tour in Scotland—save indeed for the pedestrian, who, in noble independence, can strike up mountain glens or lose himself on untrodden heights at his own sweet will. But the truth is that the coach routes, and to some extent the railroads also, traverse much of the finest scenery of the country. The admirable roads constructed through the Highlands by General Wade's soldiers in the early part of the last century (1726–1737) were but the beginning of a system by which the Highlands have been pierced in almost all directions, and wild regions opened up once declared inaccessible. On General Wade's bridge over the river Tay, a somewhat grandiloquent inscription was placed in good Latin, which may be Englished thus :

" Behold with wonder this Military Way, extended by various Passes, 250 miles beyond the Roman limits : triumphing over fens and morasses ; levelled through rocks and mountains, and carried on, as you now see it, in spite of the River Tay (*indignanti Tavo*). This arduous work, G. Wade, commander of the forces in Scotland, brought to perfection by his great judgment and ten years' labour of his soldiers in the year of our Lord 1738. Of such mighty efficacy are the Royal Auspices of George the Second ! "

A more expressive tribute to what was really a great enterprise was in the distich, rather Hibernian than Scottish in tone :

" Had you seen these roads before they were made,
You'd lift up your hands and bless General Wade ! "

The railroads, too, in some of the fairest and grandest scenes of Scotland, cannot be said even by the most determined votaries of the picturesque to have destroyed the charm. In truth, the thin line creeping along the margin of some stupendous mountain, as in the Pass of Brander, or along Glen Ogle, or amid the heights encircling Strathpeffer, is altogether too inconsiderable to disturb the effect of the scenery. There is nothing intrusive, as there would be, for instance, in many parts of the English Lake District : while, for the travellers themselves, I do not know journeys more replete with charm than the railway routes from Callander to Oban, or from Dingwall to Strome Ferry. Parts of the Highland railway, especially in its downward slope, where it skirts the river Spey, are also surpassingly beautiful. On the whole, the tourist has reason to be grateful for the facilities provided, and the votary of the beautiful may restrain his protest.

Yet of course the paths which lie away from the possibilities of travel by railroad or by coach, will to many form the greatest attraction, as they have the most inexhaustible variety. The Highlands of Scotland have always something new, in every direction, no matter how often the visitor may have explored their recesses. Few persons who have not travelled in this country have any idea of the immense multitude of the mountain heights, of the lochs and glens and streams. Every one knows about Ben Nevis and Ben Lomond ; but there are more than *twenty* mountains intervening between these two in height. Lochnagar has been made familiar by Byron's poem and by association with Her Majesty's Highland home : Cairngorm, again, is known to have something to do with pebbles : but who, except those who have wandered among the Grampians, have any idea of Brae-Riach or Ben Muich-Dhui ? Yet these, with Ben Lawers, Ben More, Ben Cruachan, Schiehallion, Ben Wyvis and Ben Vorlich, all surpass Ben Lomond in height, and all have grandeurs and beauties of their own. Then there are the countless lower hill-ranges, often surpassing their mightier brethren in grace of outline and in woodland richness. The "waters" that spring from their slopes and become tributary to one or

JOHN KNOX—(*from the Painting in the National Portrait Gallery*).

other of the great rivers that seek the German Ocean—the Forth, the Tay, the Dee, the Spey—have many a nook of inexpressible charm, while the broad "straths," through which these rivers pursue the lower part of their course, are lovely in their luxuriance. Many a loch and lochlet too, besides these which every one visits, have beauties little if at all inferior : and how numerous are these sheets of water may be seen in the *Sportsman's Guide*, which contains the names of 1037 separate lochs—many of them, no doubt, mere tarns among the hills ; and of 1166 rivers, large and small.

In the Lowlands, also, there are some Highland beauties, as shown farther on in this book, with many a charm peculiar to themselves. In fact, it is impossible to select a tour which shall not have its fascinations to lovers of the beautiful. Of the historical and antiquarian interest attached to many spots, little need be said. Some of these associations will be found touched upon in the following pages: but the topic would require a volume to itself. A few renowned names, ancient and modern, necessarily occur in any book that treats on Scotland; Knox and Scott and Burns could not fail of mention: nor, on other grounds, Mary Queen of Scots, nor the young "Pretender." But such references are fragmentary, and connected chiefly with localities that suggest the names.

Nor have we attempted to sketch the character of the Scottish people, with personal anecdotes and reminiscences. Other writers have done this with distinguished success; and after Dean Ramsay, and one or two who have followed him, there can be little to say. This volume of *Pictures* is intended to deal chiefly with external aspects, such as might strike any observant traveller. No one indeed can fail to be struck with certain salient peculiarities, such as a bluntness and independence, which mean not rudeness, but genuine respect to the worthy, with a caution that is not cunning because it is so frank, and withal a genuine, kindly humour. I know indeed that high authorities have denied to Caledonians the credit of wit. Has it not been said, "It requires a surgical operation to get a joke into a Scotchman?" "Maybe," retorted one, "it was an *English* joke that Mr. Smith was meaning!" A high intelligence will be found in all classes—the result in part of the school system which has prevailed in Scotland through many generations, and in part of the Biblical training of the people through the ministrations of their churches, and the general familiarity with the dialectics of ecclesiastical and theological controversy. This familiarity no doubt has its unfavourable side: but, on the whole, it has deepened seriousness and quickened intelligence. A stranger in one of the towns soon feels in little things that he has reached a higher level. The first man of whom he asks his way will probably direct him according to the points of the compass. "Go a hundred yards farther to the west: then take the turn to the north," and so on. I have, on the other hand, repeatedly directed London cabmen to set me down on the north side of St. Paul's Churchyard, and the general reply has been, "Which side is that, Sir, right or left?" No Scotch driver would ever be at such a loss in Edinburgh or Glasgow, Dundee or Aberdeen.

The reader may probably expect to find the volume, like others treating of Scotland, embellished with peculiarities of dialect. These have, however, been purposely disregarded. Masters of the art, like Burns, Scott, or, I may add, Dr. George Macdonald, may indulge this freedom. An Englishman generally fails; and to a practised Scottish eye, the "dialect" appears only a series of awkward misspellings. What is gained by writing *lang* for *long*, *aits* for *oats*, or even *fa'* for *fall?* Possibly the *maybe*, in the little criticism just quoted on Sydney Smith, ought to have been *aiblins;* but it is best to write only in a tongue of which one is sure. At the same time there are words in constant Scottish use which can never sound even to our ears quite like their English synonyms. A *brae* is more than a *slope*, and a *loch* is different somehow from a *lake* (apart from the application of the word to an inlet of the sea); *laverock* is a more musical name than *lark*, *lintie* than linnet; *gowan* than *daisy:* the *birks* of Aberfeldy suggest to us more than the Aberfeldy *birchtrees;* while the fond charm of the *bonnie wee* thing has almost evaporated in *little* and *pretty*. We do not pretend to account for this; the fact is certainly so. I shall not soon forget the sense of strangeness with which I once saw the word *brae* applied to a steep, unsavoury street in the closest part of Glasgow. It seemed a desecration!

But on the tempting subject of language we must not now enter. One interesting application of the topic will be the elucidation of many hundreds of proper names; but for this the excellent Glossaries given by Murray, Black, or Baddeley must be consulted. There is a history in these Gaelic and Norse appellations; as interesting and suggestive in its way as we have in another set of words relating to articles in common use, and pointing to olden connections between Scotland and France; an association to which perhaps few give any thought when they call an earthern dish an *ashet* (assiette), or speak of a leg of mutton as a *jigget* (gigot).

It only remains to express the cordial acknowledgments of the writer and of the Tract Society to Messrs. Valentine & Co., Dundee, for allowing to their draughtsmen the use of their excellent photographs, in sketching the frontispiece to this work, as also the views of the Trossachs (p. 98), of Oban (p. 64), and of John O'Groats (p. 194). A similar permission has been as kindly granted by Messrs. G. W. Wilson & Co., Aberdeen, for permission to copy their view of the Martyrs' Memorial in the Greyfriars' Churchyard, Edinburgh (p. 42), to employ their photograph of Ben Nevis (p. 78), and to use some of their Ross and Sutherlandshire views in the last chapter.

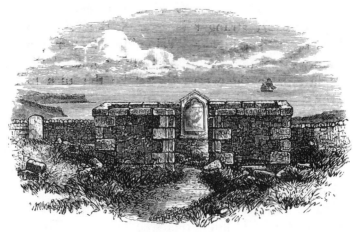

KILMUIR KIRKYARD, SKYE (WHERE FLORA MACDONALD WAS BURIED).

LASSWADE CHURCH.

BALMORAL FROM THE MEADOWS.

List of Illustrations.

ACROSS THE BORDER: TO EDINBURGH AND GLASGOW.

GLIMPSES OF EDINBURGH AND GLASGOW.

BY THE CLYDE, TO THE WESTERN COAST.

THROUGH THE WESTERN HIGHLANDS.

THE CENTRAL HIGHLANDS: STIRLING TO INVERNESS.

THE EASTERN COAST AND DEESIDE.

TO THE FAR NORTH.

AILSA CRAIG.

"IN the history of Scotland, too, I can find properly but one epoch: we may say, it contains nothing of world-interest at all but this Reformation by Knox. A poor barren country, full of continual broils, dissensions, massacrings; a people in the last state of rudeness and destitution, little better perhaps than Ireland at this day. Hungry fierce barons, not so much as able to form any arrangement with each other *how to divide* what they fleeced from these poor drudges; but obliged, as the Columbian Republics are at this day, to make of every alteration a revolution; no way of changing a ministry but by hanging the old ministers on gibbets: this is a historical spectacle of no very singular significance! 'Bravery' enough, I doubt not; fierce fighting in abundance: but not braver or fiercer than that of their old Scandinavian Sea-king ancestors; *whose* exploits we have not found worth dwelling on! It is a country as yet without a soul: nothing developed in it but what is rude, external, semi-animal. And now at the Reformation, the internal life is kindled, as it were, under the ribs of this outward material death. A cause, the noblest of causes kindles itself, like a beacon set on high; high as Heaven, yet attainable from Earth;—whereby the meanest man becomes not a Citizen only, but a Member of Christ's visible Church; a veritable Hero, if he prove a true man!"

"This that Knox did for his Nation, I say, we may really call a resurrection as from death. It was not a smooth business; but it was welcome surely, and cheap at that price, had it been far rougher. On the whole, cheap at any price;—as life is. The people began to *live*: they needed first of all to do that, at what cost and costs soever. Scotch Literature and Thought, Scotch Industry; James Watt, David Hume, Walter Scott, Robert Burns: I find Knox and the Reformation acting in the heart's core of every one of these persons and phenomena; I find that without the REFORMATION they would not have been."

CARLYLE'S *Lectures on Heroes and Hero Worship*, IV.

ACROSS THE BORDER:
TO EDINBURGH AND GLASGOW.

BOTHWELL CASTLE, ON THE CLYDE.

THE BRAES OF YARROW.

ACROSS THE BORDER: TO EDINBURGH AND GLASGOW.

ROSLIN CASTLE.

FOR practical purposes, a pleasure tour in Scotland generally begins with Edinburgh or Glasgow. Travellers are too much in haste to reach the Highlands to spare time for the Border, renowned though it be in song and story; or to take any leisurely survey of the country that lies between the last towns left on the English side, and the two great Scottish cities. Yet this country is worth visiting in every part of it, for its own sake, and for that of its memories. Draw a straight line across from Greenock to Leith, and south of it, from east to west, will be found much, if not most, that is associated with the chief glories of Scotland. The tourist may well then linger; and it is hard to say which particular route will prove of the highest interest. There is the Eastern line, by the coast of the Firth of Forth: and the Western, which crosses the Solway Frith near Carlisle.

Travellers again by the latter may strike across to Edinburgh by the "Waverley Route," or may follow the course of the infant Clyde by way of Carstairs Junction, or may take the South-western line to Glasgow by the dales of the Annan and the Nith. We have travelled by all these lines in turn, and have found in every one a special charm. In picturesqueness perhaps the palm must be conceded to the route by the East coast, on which, from the first glimpse of Berwick-upon-Tweed, with its encircling wall, its high red roofs, and its houses seeming from the railway above to be crowded together on the steep river's bank, every mile is full of charm; especially where the line is carried along the verge of the cliff, with the noble expanse of the German Ocean full in view, or where, diverging inland, it passes through the rich pastures and great cornfields of Haddingtonshire (or East Lothian[1]), throughout which, down to the close-cropped hedges, economising arable space, everything speaks of high farming on a kindly soil.

The traveller may do worse than stay for a night, or, as the writer did on one occasion, pass a quiet Sabbath, at DUNBAR, with its old shattered castle on a rocky brow, in which time and weather and the hand of man have wrought such havoc, that it is hard to distinguish the foundations of the fabric from the rugged cliff, or to decide which of the underground recesses are ocean-hollowed caves, and which are ancient castle crypts. Here was spent the strange sad honeymoon of Bothwell and Mary: and with this the history of the fortress really ends, as the pile was soon afterwards reduced to a ruin by the Queen's half-brother, the Regent Murray. The precincts of the castle now form a fine recreation ground for the week-day use of the people: on the Sabbath, it was observable that chains were drawn across the swing-gates at the entrances—showing that we were in Scotland. The chains, however, it may be remarked, were there rather by way of testimony, than as a material hindrance; not a few graceless urchins having climbed over them, without let or hindrance, into the enclosure. But upon the whole, the stillness and peacefulness of the day were very refreshing. I remarked here, what afterwards became so noticeable in many a Scottish town, the peculiar resonant tramp of feet on the pavement at the time of the services. There was little or no sound of wheels to break the effect, rendered more impressive by the contrast of the previous silence. It was pleasant to join in the worship of the Free Church, led by a pastor, hale though venerable, who had been one of the seceders in 1843, and had ever since that stormy time held on his useful way in this quiet little town. In the course of the services there was a pathetic allusion to the fewness of the survivors of that great conflict. Some of us remember it all so well, and it is already history! These forty years, it is not too much to say, have revolutionised the religious life of Scotland; not simply by the organisation and the vigorous work of

[1] Englishmen are often perplexed about the Lothians, especially at election-times. Is it superfluous to inform some readers that Haddingtonshire is East Lothian, Linlithgowshire West Lothian, and Edinburghshire Mid Lothian?

4

another ecclesiastical community, but by the new vigour inbreathed into all the churches.

Much in the neighbourhood of Dunbar invited a longer stay, had it been possible. To the south-east there is the undulating pastoral district of Lammermoor—scene of Sir Walter Scott's most tragic story, the localities of which are all duly pointed out. Wolf's Crag, the home of the Master of

DUNBAR CASTLE.

Ravenswood, famous for the humours and the devices of Caleb Balderstone, is unquestionably recognisable in Fast Castle, on a wild promontory to the east. Not far from the town again is the battle-field, where, in 1650, Cromwell defeated the Scottish army, under General Leslie. Readers of Carlyle's *Cromwell* will recollect the careful accuracy with which the locality is sketched :

5

"The small town of Dunbar stands high and windy, looking down over its herring-boats, over its grim old castle, now much honey-combed, on one of those projecting rock-promontories with which that shore of the Firth of Forth is niched and vandyked, as far as the eye can reach. A beautiful sea; good land too, now that the plougher understands his trade; a grim niched barrier of whinstone sheltering it from the chafings and tumblings of the big blue German Ocean. Seaward, St. Abb's Head, of whinstone, bounds your horizon to the east, not very far off; west, close by, is the deep bay and fishy little village of Belhaven, the gloomy Bass and other rock islets, and farther the hills of Fife and foreshadows of the Highlands are visible as you look seaward. From the bottom of Belhaven Bay, to that of the next sea-bight St. Abb's-ward, the town and its environs form a peninsula. Along the base of which peninsula, 'not much above a mile and a half from sea to sea,' Oliver Cromwell's army, on Monday, the 2nd of September, 1650, stands ranked, with its tents and town behind it—in very forlorn circumstances." [1]

The description, as we know from Carlyle's biography, was the result of careful personal examination, and in the *Letters of Mrs. Carlyle* we read of the author's visit, and his windy walk over the high plain. Equally striking is the battle picture. " 'I never saw such a charge of foot and horse,' says one; nor did I. Oliver was still near to Yorkshire Hodgson, when the shock succeeded. Hodgson heard them say, 'They run! I profess they run.' And over St. Abb's Head, and the German Ocean, just then, bursts the first gleam of the level sun upon us, 'and I heard Nol say, in the words of the Psalmist, "Let God arise, let His enemies be scattered,"' or in Rous's metre,

'Let God arise, and scatterèd
Let all His enemies be;
And let all those that do Him hate
Before His presence flee!'

"Even so, the Scotch army is shivered to utter ruin; rushes in tumultuous wreck, hither, thither, to Belhaven, or, in their distraction, even to Dunbar; the chase goes as far as Haddington, led by Hacker. 'The Lord General made a halt,' says Hodgson, 'and sang the hundred and seventeenth psalm,' till our horse could gather for the chase. Hundred and seventeenth psalm, at the foot of the Doon hill. Then we uplift it, to the tune of Bangor, or some still higher score, and roll it strong and great against the sky:

'O give ye praise unto the Lord
All nati-ons that be
Likewise ye people all, accord
His name to magnify!

For great to us-ward ever are
His loving-kindnesses;
His truth endures for evermore;
The Lord O do ye bless.'

"And now, to the chase again!"

[1] *Oliver Cromwell's Letters and Speeches, with Elucidations.* Introduction to Letters cxxxix.–cxlvi.

From the painting]

THE BASS ROCK : WAITING FOR THE HOMEWARD BOUND.

[by Colin Hunter.

The remembrance of it survives in the local popular name of the battle : *Tuesday's Race*, from the day of the week on which it was fought, and from the hurry of the flight and pursuit which followed.

Out at sea the Bass Rock is grandly in sight, and those who have visited it describe the excursion as very pleasant. The enormous flight of sea-birds when disturbed by visitors or by the firing of a gun, is very wonderful. The ruins of Tantallon Castle occupy a rocky promontory nearly opposite, and at a short distance from the pretty sea-bathing resort of North Berwick. Apparently corresponding to the Bass Rock are the inland craggy hills peculiar to this district, and termed *Laws*. North Berwick Law is one of the most commanding of these heights. Traprain Law is another,

THE BASS ROCK : DISTANT VIEW.

near Linton station, inland, and not far from Hailes Castle, where Mary and Bothwell lived for a time before the surrender of the former at Carberry Hill. The country people say that the name "Traprain Law" was derived from this capture, as it was thereabouts that *la reine* was *trapped*. Not a bad illustration of the way in which etymologies are made!

Nearer Edinburgh, on the same line, is another battle-field, at which we may pause with interest. It is at Preston Pans (the *pans*, for getting salt by evaporation) where Prince Charles Stuart defeated the King's troops under Sir John Cope, on the 21st of September, 1745. It was chiefly this delusive gleam of success which encouraged the Young Pretender to march southward, to his ruin ; but the chief interest of the scene to ourselves is that Colonel James Gardiner fell in the skirmish, for it was little more. We give a sketch of his monument, as it stands on the field. To this day the life of Gardiner by Dr. Doddridge remains one of the finest portraitures we

TANTALLON CASTLE.

possess of a type of character very real, and happily not infrequent in our day—the brave and humble-minded Christian soldier. And Sir Walter Scott, in *Waverley*, has done more justice to this brave God-fearing man than to some other of his Puritan heroes.

Soon after leaving Preston Pans the train plunges into a tunnel, from which it emerges in the ravine over which seem to tower, height beyond height, the massive buildings of EDINBURGH. The approach is curiously unlike that to any other city; but we must not linger in the metropolis at present, for we have yet to glance at the other routes

COLONEL GARDINER'S MONUMENT.

enumerated above, at least as rich in their personal and historical associations.

Instead, then, of Berwick, we will suppose the traveller to have chosen Carlisle as his starting-point, and to have fixed upon the Waverley Route, as the railway company has named it in memory of Scott. After crossing and recrossing the Esk, a little above the Solway Firth, the line runs up Liddisdale, undulating and beautifully wooded, with glimpses of distant hills:

then for mile after mile, after crossing the Border at Kershopefoot, in long sweeps and curves traverses the bare pastoral Cheviots, whose vast rounded summits and grassy slopes fill up the whole field of view; only a few clumps of fir-trees appearing here and there at the bottom of the dells, where scanty streams pursue their way. Just before reaching Hawick, where we cross the Teviot, Branksome Tower is passed on the left; still beyond is

MELROSE ABBEY, FROM THE RIVER.

the Vale of Ettrick, famous for "the Shepherd," James Hogg, who was a very real personage in his day, though Professor Wilson in the *Noctes Ambrosianæ*, did his best to render his honest friend a mythical personage. Still farther again is the Yarrow, with its "dowie dens," famous in Scottish pastoral poetry, but better known to us in three lovely poems of Wordsworth.

At Ettrick, too, lie the remains of an author whose work, now perhaps

12

little read, used to be the great "Sunday book" in grave Scottish house-holds during several generations—Thomas Boston, the writer of the *Fourfold State*. But Ettrick and Yarrow must both remain "unvisited" by us now, as they may be better approached another time from Moffat on the west, or from Selkirk on the north, and we are nearing MELROSE, having crossed from the valley of the Teviot to that of the Tweed; and we shall need

DRYBURGH ABBEY.

all the time at disposal for the Abbey, for Abbotsford and for Dryburgh.

To describe "fair Melrose" would be superfluous. The impression even of a first visit is that we have seen it before, so vividly has it been brought before us both by poet and artist. Its position, close upon the outskirts of the little town, does not destroy, but rather enhances its charm. Instead of finding it, like Tintern, or like Furness, in the heart of a romantic valley, we enter it direct from a modern street, to be plunged at once into its solemn stillness, and awed by the glimpses of its old-world beauty, still most apparent amid the restorations, in which different ages have by turns displayed their sense of the fitness of things! To see it by moonlight is of course the ambition of every tourist, the achievement of but few; and it has been said that Scott himself never visited it at this witching time, having evolved the description which has enraptured so many by its accuracy as well as by its loveliness, entirely from his own imagination.

Two roads from Melrose attract the traveller almost equally; the one, westward, to Abbotsford, the other in the opposite direction, to Dryburgh Abbey. Happily, on the occasion of my visit, there was time for both, in a long summer day's leisurely survey. The walk to Dryburgh was somewhat long, and might have been saved in great part by taking the train back to St. Boswell's, the station passed before reaching Melrose. But the way was

ABBOTSFORD.

very beautiful, including one magnificent view of the Tweed, with its wooded banks. The ruin itself is not extensive, but the aisle in which Scott lies buried is surely the ideal of a poet's resting-place. His beloved Tweed half encircles the spot, the ruin is embosomed in fair trees, while the broken walls, still noble in their decay, are more appropriately and solemnly suggestive than the stateliest mausoleum could have been. The remains of Sir Walter Scott are there among those of his kindred—his wife, his eldest son, and his son-in-law and biographer, Mr. Lockhart. The guardian of the ruins also will not fail to point out the tombstone of Henry Erskine, whose sons, Ralph and Ebenezer, founded in 1740 the

ABBOTSFORD : THE DRAWING-ROOM.

Secession Church of Scotland, now merged in the United Presbyterian body.

But the journey to Abbotsford remained. Probably the natural order would have been to visit the home which Scott occupied in his lifetime before this pilgrimage to his grave. Why a different course of proceeding was adopted need not be explained; I did not regret it afterwards, when even after having duly inspected all the relics so lovingly preserved and so courteously shown, the deepest impression left was still that of the quiet, lovely tomb. The visitor cannot choose but look with interest on Abbotsford as the poet's chosen home—a noble residence and beautiful for situation, although lower in the valley than modern taste approves. It might be ungenerous to ask whether the rearing of this lordly abode was worth the toil and struggle that it entailed; the world at least is the richer for those stupendous intellectual labours which at length, though slowly, exhausted the poet's life. There still we find ourselves in the very scene of these great achievements. The Library contains his books as he left them: in the study there is the writing-table where he used to sit, the desk at which he wrote, and which was closed when he ceased, more than half a century ago. The quaint suits of armour that he loved to collect are where he left them; but their sight awakens no enthusiasm now for the days of ancient chivalry. That passion seems extinct; new habits of thought have succeeded, and not the greatest of novelists would venture, if he could, to give to the reader of this

ABBOTSFORD : THE STUDY.

15

generation another *Ivanhoe*. From casque and mail, the visitor turns to the homely memorial of the man himself; his coat and hat and stick, preserved with reverent affection. Yet these vestiges of life seemed only to make the fact of death more near: and there was a deeper interest in yonder quiet Abbey, and in the words of Christian faith and hope upon the poet's tomb. Still it was something to have seen even the books and the writing-desk; for everything connected with the daily habits of a great man tends to illuminate his biography, and in some measure to increase our interest in the works in which his spirit most truly lives among men.

ABBOTSFORD : THE LIBRARY.

After Melrose there is little of interest immediately bordering the Waverley Route, unless indeed the traveller can spare time to change at Galashiels into a line which will take him to Edinburgh by a more circuitous course, passing from the valley of the Tweed (which it follows upwards as far as Peebles) to the dale of the North Esk, with the wonderfully beautiful ravine of Hawthornden and the famous Roslin Chapel.

ABBOTSFORD : THE ARMOURY.

The visit will in most cases be made from Edinburgh: but the traveller who is not incommoded by luggage may save time by calling there on his northward journey. He must stop at Hawthornden station, from which it is an easy walk to the entrance of the grounds. Here lived the poet Drummond, so famous in his day that Ben Jonson travelled on foot from London to Scotland, chiefly, it is said, to converse with him. But his melancholy strains are now little read; and to most visitors the beauty of the place c

HAWTHORNDEN.

is more than the fame of the inhabitant. We do not say, "It was here that Drummond lived," but, "It was Drummond who lived here." The house is sufficiently picturesque—a mansion of the seventeenth century upon a grey cliff towering above the glen, with the ruined fragment of a tower hard by. But the beauty of the scene is in the glen itself, to which we descend through prettily laid out grounds, noting, as we pass, the caverns in the rock beneath the house, constructed with evident care in ancient times for some unknown purpose; also, "Ben Jonson's Tree," the "Poet Drummond's Seat," and "John Knox's Pulpit." These may be more or less apocryphal; but there is no doubt about the charm of the deep glen where the stream, albeit defiled by the works of man, pursues its way between broken cliffs and overhanging woods. It is the sense of nearness to busy manufactures and great cities in this romantic and apparently sequestered spot, that either heightens or destroys the charm, according to the spectator's mood. He will have abundant time to decide whether the sense of beauty or of incongruity is the stronger; as, after crossing the little bridge from Hawthornden grounds, it is a long walk up the valley to Roslin, which he must also see. The regular plan is to climb from the glen to the castle, approached by a lofty bridge, and to recross to the chapel. We venture to suggest that the castle may well be omitted, as, apart from the view of the glen from the rocky platform on which the ruin stands, there is neither picturesqueness nor real historic interest to repay the visitor. The chapel, situated on the high ground beyond, overlooking the castle, must by all means be examined, as an almost unique specimen of decorative art applied to somewhat heavy architecture. It is a small building, massive in its details, with a general impression of heaviness that the splendid and even excessive ornamentation but serves to relieve. Had the structure been completed according to the original design, in which this chapel was but the choir of a great collegiate church, the magnificence would have seemed more in place. The chapel is now fitted up with seats, has an organ gallery at the western end, and is used for the worship of the Scottish Episcopal Church. The 'Prentice Pillar, with its wreathed-work of foliage, will of course be noted by the visitor; and the custodian of the place tells the story effectively, as he has rehearsed it a thousand times. Is there any one of our readers who has not heard it? In the temporary absence of the master-builder, an apprentice, essaying his hand upon a portion of the fabric, so far surpassed him in skill that the jealous and exasperated master struck the youth dead upon the spot. The story, however, is found in various forms, but with the same main incident, in many ages, and in relation to different walks of art. The incident probably springs from fable, so true to human nature that it has been accepted as an "ower true tale," and shows to us how myths are made.

Leaving the chapel we find ourselves in the little village of Roslin, or Rosslyn, as it seems now generally to be written, and at about seven minutes' distance the pedestrian may reach the railway station for Edinburgh. There are, however, very few trains in the day, and careful arrangement is necessary that time may not be vexatiously thrown away in a place where, after the glen and the chapel, there is literally nothing to see. Part of the

ROSLIN CHAPEL, WITH THE 'PRENTICE PILLAR.

interest of this excursion, no doubt, as Sir Walter Scott long ago remarked, is that its picturesque features form so sudden and unexpected a contrast to the surrounding country. In the Highlands few persons would take the trouble to walk up this glen, but its nearness to Edinburgh, and the neighbourhood of Roslin, attract crowds of visitors every summer. Still farther south, below the south-eastern slopes of the Pentland Hills, is the yet more romantic glen of Habbie's Howe, with its waterfall, supposed to

HABBIE'S HOWE.

have suggested the description in Ramsay's *Gentle Shepherd;* and the whole surrounding region is full of pastoral and sylvan beauty.

Returning, however, to Carlisle: there are two other railway routes of great interest, and more direct, at least in their access to Glasgow. They unitedly traverse the old Solway Moss, once the notorious haunt of freebooters, and pass through the flat "debateable ground" where, until the union of the two kingdoms, bold maurauders bade defiance to the laws of both, until the little river Sark is crossed, and the train reaches Gretna Green, once famous for runaway weddings. The idea of making the Scottish marriage law available to fugitives from England, seems to have first occurred to a man named Paisley, residing here about 1760; Gretna being fixed upon as near the Border, though, of course, any other part of Scotland would have answered the purpose; and it was not until 1856 that the usage was stopped by Act of Parliament, requiring previous residence as a condition of marriage. The country now has but little attraction; once it was a vast forest, but in the days of Border rapine the wood was cleared away to destroy the haunts of the moss-troopers, and it is now for the most part a bare open plain. On the left is Annandale, where Edward Irving spent his youthful days; and some twelve miles from the Border the traveller reaches Ecclefechan, an uninteresting-looking village, but famous for the birth of Thomas Carlyle. His father's strong-built house stands there as when the sturdy God-fearing Scottish peasant put his best work into its stone walls. Truly, whatever else may be thought of Carlyle's *Reminiscences*, the pictures of his father and mother as there delineated, will live as long as the fame of their illustrious son shall last. The type of man is familiar to all who have watched the stalwart shepherd tramping over the hills with his colley by his side, or who have stopped for a little talk with a fisherman on the shore, or who have joined the group of country folk on the mountain side as they wended their way on the Sabbath morning to the humble house of prayer; but Carlyle has disclosed the secret of its inner nobleness, and has shown to us how a living faith, with that true humility that does not shrink from self-assertion where it is right, creates the true heroic character. Carlyle could hardly have written his *Cromwell* so sympathetically, had he not known his father so well. And who is not touched by the picture of that peasant mother, with her anxious cares for her son, denying herself and caring for all his little material comforts, that he might be able to climb to a level whither her earnest spirit could not follow him, save with anxious longings for his spiritual welfare! To read those simple-hearted letters of hers is infinitely touching, and we do not wonder that the son who cherished them and gave them to the world after more than half a century, with all the scorn and bitterness with which he looked upon men in general, and especially on those who have found a deeper secret in life than his own, could not but believe in the truth and goodness embodied in the belief, the work and the worship of that lowly home.

But we must pass from Ecclefechan, over the district where the line

STONEBYRES FALLS.

climbs upwards along the banks of the Annan, to Beattock, from which station a line is now opened to Moffat, a charming little watering-place among streams and wooded hills, overtopped by the Hartfell range, the highest in Southern Scotland. There is a pleasant drive to the Spa, with excursions to the waterfall called the Grey Mare's Tail, and to the dark, desolate Loch Skene from which it issues; or, through a cleft in the mountains beyond the cascade, to St. Mary's Loch upon the Yarrow. Or, diverging before the waterfall is reached, the traveller may pierce the hill-range to the right into the Ettrick valley. The air is most pure and exhilarating, and, in addition to the ordinary watering-place accommodations, a large Hydropathic Establishment has been opened here, as at Melrose, Crieff, Dunblane, Pitlochrie, Callander, Bridge of Allan, Rothesay, Forres, and many other places of popular resort in Scotland.

We resume our journey from the Beattock junction, and having now crossed the watershed at the height of about a thousand feet above the sea, soon discern a narrow stream making its way with many a winding over the green moor. This is the CLYDE, which we cross and recross before reaching the junction at Carstairs, whence radiate lines to Edinburgh, to Glasgow, to Stirling, and the North. It will be a pity, however, not to stay at least for two or three hours to see LANARK and the Falls of the Clyde. The town itself has little that is interesting, unless we are moved by curiosity or by old association to visit the settlement in which Robert Owen, nearly a hundred years ago, strove to organise industry, and to inaugurate a new moral world. The parallelograms and manufactories of the Socialist schemes failed, as might have been expected; but there was some germ of practical wisdom in his choice of a locality, since the mills of New Lanark, now, I believe, the property of Manchester manufacturers, are thriving and successful, while the aspect of regularity and good order which they present may be in some measure due to the projector's plans. But we must hurry on to the waterfalls, which may perhaps impress us all the more because the glen in which they make their grand successive descents is surrounded by few accessories of beauty of any kind. The country, to say the truth, is uninteresting until the river is reached, but the three falls are magnificent. Corra Linn, the central one, nearest to New Lanark, is the finest; but Bonnington Linn, the highest, divided into two parts, with a rocky island between—a miniature Schaffhausen—is also imposing, and Stonebyres, three miles from Lanark, by the road-side, with its surroundings of cliff and foliage, is also well worth visiting. The tourist will probably see no finer waterfalls than these three until he reaches Foyers on Loch Ness.

The railway journey from Carstairs to Edinburgh has no points of special interest; that to Glasgow gives the opportunity, by a very slight détour, of visiting Hamilton Palace, once famous for its art-treasures, and

25

still sumptuous, although despoiled. More attractive, however, will be the remains of the old Caledonian Forest, where the celebrated herd of Scotch wild cattle still roam at large, with the ruins of Cadzow Castle, the ancient Hamilton Palace, commemorated by Sir Walter Scott. Very near also is "Bothwell Brig," where the Covenanters were defeated by the Duke of Monmouth and Claverhouse, on the 22nd of June, 1679, as described in *Old Mortality*. But these scenes of historic interest will, perhaps, be better visited from Glasgow, than taken on the way to the city. A day could scarcely be better spent than in traversing them.

The last of the alternative routes to Glasgow, as mentioned above, denominated the "South Western," is more circuitous than that just described, but derives a special interest from its giving the tourist an opportunity of visiting, at small expenditure of time, the land of Burns. Turning aside at Gretna, the line passes through Annan, where it crosses the river, and at Dumfries reaches the Nith, up which it pursues its way. For lovely glimpses of hill and woodland, with fertile cornfields and pastures between, and the gleaming river amidst them all, there can hardly be a pleasanter summer evening's journey than this. At least, so I found it, after a long morning of wonderful interest spent at DUMFRIES, beginning, of course, with a visit to the cemetery where, beyond a crowd of monuments, stands the mausoleum over the poet's grave. Much cannot be said for the monument itself. It is a poor Grecian temple, glazed between the columns, and the allegorical design—the genius of Scotland casting her mantle over the ploughman—has a common-place effect. The attempt at classic forms and figures seemed in truth singularly infelicitous; though it could not but be deeply interesting, apart from all such accessories, to know that here was the last earthly resting-place of Burns, the poet to whom, with Cowper and Wordsworth, each according to his special genius, belongs the distinction of having so widened the domain of poetry as to include the commonest interests and homeliest cares that touch the heart of man. I might have gone to see the house in which Burns spent his last days, and which still has much to remind the visitor of the poet; but time pressed, and I was bent on another errand. For Dumfries is famous in the annals of martyrdom. In the cemetery itself, a plain obelisk marks the grave of some who suffered in 1667. A lovely drive by Annan Water brought me to Irongray Church, near which, among overshadowing trees, is the grave of two others, with the quaint inscription :

> " By Legg and Bloodie Bruce commands
> We were hung up by hellish hands ;
> And so, their furious wrath to stay,
> We died near Kirk of Irongray ;
> And boundless peace we now partake
> For freedom's and religion's sake."

Near this church also is the tomb of Helen Walker, the original of Jeanie Deans, with an inscription written by Sir Walter Scott.

But I had not yet finished with the Covenanters' memorials; as perhaps the most interesting of all was one among the hills, not to be discovered without difficulty—a long drive, then an ascent through a rugged lane, and a walk over a piece of barren undulating moorland, with much climbing over stone fences. The place was well adapted in its seclusion for a solemn service held there in the summer of 1678, when for the last time a band of Covenanting brethren met together to celebrate the Lord's Supper. Then they parted, some to fall in battle, others to suffer on the gibbet, few to survive the conflict of that terrible time, but all to hold fast by the faith to which they then renewed their solemn pledge. It is no wonder that this bleak spot is regarded with affectionate veneration, the very stones which served for the table and for seats in the service being marked as the Communion Stones of Irongray. But, lest the outward features of the scene should become obliterated or unrecognizable, a simple monument, surmounted by the representation of the Cup, has been raised in recent years; and in all Scotland there was no memorial that was so deeply impressive to me as this emblem of our faith and hope, with all its sacred and stern associations, on those lonely moorland hills!

Near the head of Nithsdale may be visited another "Martyrs' Grave," not far from Cumnock; but that I did not stay to see. The country has many

COVENANTERS' MONUMENT.

such memorials; and not far off is the battle-field of Drumclog, where the Covenanters gained a temporary success, June 1, 1679, three weeks before the rout of Bothwell Bridge. But the neighbourhood of AYR attracted me again a little from the direct line, to visit Alloway Kirk, the "Twa Brigs," the birthplace and the monument of Burns. The South-western line may be left for this purpose at Mauchline, about twelve miles from Ayr. After a night in Ayr, I took a stroll through its streets to the two bridges, auld and new, celebrated in Burns's *Dialogue*, then down to the steam-wharf, and found that preparations, which I afterwards learned were made almost daily through the summer, were in full readiness to conduct expected visitors to the shrine.   As soon as the boat from Glasgow arrived, a stream of waggonettes and other "machines" started in full procession through the town.   I followed on foot; there was no mistaking the way!   After a somewhat uninteresting walk of two miles, I reached the poet's birth-place—an unpretending cottage in front, a gaudy drinking-saloon behind, probably erected over the cottage-

THE MARTYRS' GRAVE.

garden for the reception of visitors, a crowd of whom had evidently just left. The saloon is hung with pictures representing scenes from the poet's works. About half a mile farther on, a flight of steps leads through a gap in a wall to a small roofless building, the ruin of "Alloway's auld kirk."   Here are the tombstones of Burns's father and mother, with a new one to the poet's sister, Mrs. Begg.   The new church—a somewhat florid Gothic structure—

is on the other side of the road. The monument stands high beyon d. There is, it must be confessed, something very striking in this memorial to the poet, whatever may be thought of its good taste or appropriateness. The nine Corinthian columns that support the circular structure are said to be emblematic of the nine muses. In a chamber within are copies of the

ON THE DOON.

chief editions of the poet's works, a bust, and a copy of the celebrated portrait by Nasmyth, with an old Bible, his last present to "Highland Mary." From the summit of the building there is a pretty view of the banks of the Doon, and of the surrounding scenery. Outside in the grounds under a canopy sit the statues of two men boozing and grinning—

Tam o' Shanter and Souter Johnnie; copies of which in clay or plaster, or carved in wood, are to be seen everywhere in the neighbourhood, for purchase, if one had a mind for such a memorial of what after every draw-back was a truly memorable visit! The tourists were found in full force around the monument, enjoying themselves according to their respective tastes, the majority, perhaps, in the inn garden, in which were seats and a summer-house, and which descends to the river; others going farther afield, down to the bank from which there is a pretty view of the old high arched bridge mentioned in *Tam o' Shanter*. A new bridge spans the stream just by the inn; and, crossing this, I found a pleasant walk back to Ayr on the other side of the river, arriving in time to reach Glasgow early in the evening.

THE AULD BRIG OF DOON.

GLIMPSES OF
EDINBURGH AND GLASGOW.

HOLYROOD PALACE AND CHAPEL, WITH ARTHUR'S SEAT.

EDINBURGH, FROM "REST AND BE THANKFUL."

GLIMPSES OF EDINBURGH AND GLASGOW.

THE first sight of EDINBURGH is something never to be forgotten. Many strangers have their earliest view of the city from the high bridge that crosses from the Old Town to the New, as they emerge from the railway station below; others, more fortunate, who have arrived after dark, or in the twilight of a summer's evening, see it for the first time from some hotel window in Princes Street commanding the long sweep of Old Edinburgh, downward from the Castle Rock, fronted by tall buildings and towers that overhang the ravine; while the slopes below are gay with grass and flowers, and Arthur's Seat beyond rears its massive head. The graceful spire of the Scott Monument forms an appropriate foreground; to the right the low colonnades of the Art Galleries close in the garden view, while to the left the eye ranges from the monuments of the Calton Hill, and the stately buildings at its foot, down to the level on which stand Holyrood Palace and Chapel; although indeed these are from many points shut out of sight by intervening buildings and the lofty North Bridge. One excellence of Edinburgh is that its plan is so simple. There is first the Old Town, Edinburgh proper—the Edinburgh of eighteenth-century writers —an immense sweep of tall houses with spires and towers interspersed, "from a palace in the plain to a castle in the air"; behind these, narrow

BIRTH-PLACE OF LORD BROUGHAM,
COWGATE, EDINBURGH.

streets, with some statelier ones, as "Chambers Street" and "Jeffrey Street," worthily preserving the names of men of whom Scotland is proud; at the back of all these one of the noblest of infirmaries, built on the "pavilion system," with its spacious grounds, and a fair walk close by; the far-famed Heriot's Hospital, and the yet more famous Greyfriars Churchyard, beside which we may descend by several different ways to the broad level Grassmarket at the foot of the precipitous Castle Rock, and return to the higher parts of the city by the Cowgate, stopping, if we please, to look at the house in which Lord Brougham was born.

It is no part of our purpose to describe the city in detail. Excellent Guide-books are to be had, and intelligent canny guides also, by those who care to be "personally conducted" from spot to spot in regulated order, and to be duly reminded of the history or the legend attached to each. But most visitors, we suspect, prefer to wander at their own will, and to select the special localities or objects to which their taste or their knowledge may attract them. The Castle is visited, of course, as much for its superb view of the city, as for anything that it contains, the Mons Meg, or even the Scottish Regalia. At the other extremity, Holyrood must also be seen, with its apartments, strangely small for royalty, its pathetic associations, and that dim stain of Rizzio's blood! The chapel behind is lovely in its ruins, though tourists often neglect it for the more easily comprehended wonders of the palace. Then, from Holyrood, few who are good walkers, or who enjoy a fine drive, will fail to ascend Arthur's Seat, where on one side they will come upon a lonely loch, to all appearance as far from the haunts of men as though it were in some Highland mountain recess; and on the other will skirt or traverse Salisbury Crags, and think of the *Heart of Mid-Lothian*. From the summit the view is fine, embracing the city outspread as a map at the beholder's feet, though too often veiled in smoke, with the Firth of Forth extending to the north and east, and in an

STAIRCASE, HOLYROOD.

CASTLE AND GRASSMARKET, EDINBURGH.

opposite direction a fair reach of country terminated by the graceful outlines of the Pentland Hills. But the city view here is less interesting on the whole than that from the Castle Rock; and the Firth of Forth with the hills of Fife behind is seen better from the Calton Hill.

In returning to the city, the tourist may pass through Newington, and by the aid of a tramcar, which seems in the great Scottish cities always at hand, may proceed along Nicolson Street for the sake of looking at least at the outside of the University Buildings and at the College of Surgeons opposite, reaching the head of Princes Street, near the Post Office, over the North Bridge. Should a keen north-east wind be blowing as he crosses this bridge, he will understand why many people inveigh against the spring climate of Edinburgh. The wind whose praises Mr. Kingsley has sung, nowhere gives a better taste of its quality than in Edinburgh, and this lofty crossing from the Old Town to the New is the very place to test it to the utter-most. Shall we look down from the North Bridge for a moment, into what we have called a ravine, where once spread the unfragrant waters of a shallow loch, but where dingy roofs of iron and glass, and long station platforms, and high flights of steps, and multitudinous branching lines of rail occupy the whole space, from tunnel to tunnel? Is it a blemish upon this noble city that the railway is thus in the very heart of it? At the first view it would appear so; and yet there

MAGDALEN CHAPEL, COWGATE, EDINBURGH.

are two sides to this question. Think of the Charing Cross Terminus and the Cannon Street Station in London, and it will appear a happy thing for the effect of Edinburgh architecture that its main railway offices are packed away, so to speak, below the general surface. Still, it is true, there is too much smoke and steam for the fair gardens that border on part of the line; but at any rate there is no obtrusive ugliness; even the spectator on the Waverley Bridge has so much to attract his upward looks in every direction that he forgets to look downwards at all! Add to this, that the traveller

37

RIDDEL'S COURT, EDINBURGH, WHERE HUME BEGAN TO WRITE HIS HISTORY.

entering Edinburgh from the south is not carried past the upper stories of mean and squalid streets, as in so many English towns and cities, but is afforded just one glimpse of Holyrood, a glance at Arthur's Seat, and is then plunged into a tunnel from which he emerges at the foot of all that is most characteristic in the architecture of the city. In this respect, therefore, the balance of advantage seems to be with the northern capital.

The Old Town, as might be expected, contains many memorials of the past, though more have disappeared. Ancient courts and wynds sufficiently illustrate the street architecture of by-gone days. Common stairs still lead—and not in these parts of the city only—to tenement above tenement, the value and the respectability diminishing with the height. To all pastoral visitation and mission work in Edinburgh and most Scottish towns, this style of building adds a toilsomeness that doubles the fatigue. It is remarkable that while the arrangement into flats seems coming into fashion in London for the middle classes, there seems a growing preference in Scotland for " self-contained houses." Certainly the great height which the former method enables architects to give the tenements for all classes is a great element in picturesqueness, and when several of these vast dwellings are lighted up at night the effect is singularly fine. There can hardly be a city in the world in which a general illumination is so imposing as it is in Edinburgh.

Of the old houses which the traveller may care to visit, none perhaps will attract him more than the manse of John Knox, still shown, in much the same state as left by the great Reformer. The quaint inscription over the lower storey: " LOFE . GOD . ABOVE . AL . AND . YOVR . NICHTBOVR . AS . YI . SELF ; " and the upward-pointing figure above the door, date, it is said, from Knox's own time. It is natural to ask for the grave of the great preacher, but the spot is uncertain. He would have no monument to commemorate his fame. No, he would be laid among his people in the old burying-place of St Giles's, and the rude inscription, " I. K. 1572," carved on a stone in the pavement of what is now Parliament Square, is the only

JOHN KNOX'S STUDY.

SIGNING THE COVENANT, GREYFRIARS CHURCHYARD.

indication of the place where his remains are supposed to rest. For the monuments of others, who after Knox's time helped to make Scotland famous, we must go to the Greyfriars Churchyard, entered through a gateway to the right after crossing the high causeway leading to the Infirmary and Heriot's Hospital, and called George the Fourth's Bridge. The large ugly building just inside the gateway is Greyfriars Church, where the National Covenant was adopted in 1638: the document was brought out into the churchyard for signature, so as to make room for the anxious crowd who pressed forward to add their names or to witness the signature of others. The stone is still pointed out—an authentic and very characteristic Scottish relic! But more impressive still are the ranges of tombs, with the names they bear of the noble and the obscure. All ranks, all characters, all creeds are here, with inscriptions, curt or elaborate, quaintly original or elegantly common-place— material enough for a biographical History of Scotland!

KNOX'S GRAVE.

The scene is one in which to spend musing hours, though destitute of the romantic accessories which tempt the sentimental traveller into many a "God's acre." The situation indeed is magnificent, beneath the Castle walls and with a grand view over the city, but nothing can be more formal than the arrangement, nor more tasteless than most of the tombs. The favourite mode of honouring the illustrious dead in this cemetery, is by enclosing a flat grave by tall iron railings, which are sometimes carried over it as well as on its three sides, the wall with its monument forming the back of the enclosure. The effect is that of a great iron cage; and many of the plots, being uncared for even to the planting of a flower, have a singularly desolate appearance. But for all that there are few, if any, places in Edinburgh to compare in true interest with this Greyfriars Churchyard. Here the persecutor and the persecuted rest together; one of the most elaborate of the

THE COVENANT STONE.

monuments is that to "Bluidy Mackenzie," as he was long called by those of whom in his lifetime he had been the terror; while the memorial to the Covenanters who suffered for their faith, many of them in the Grassmarket below, is of a touching simplicity.

If we wish to pass from these extinct forms of strife to the discussions, and often the controversies of the present, we should take care to visit

Edinburgh in May, and to secure tickets for the meetings of the three great Ecclesiastical Parliaments, the Established, the Free, and that which is universally called in Scotland the U.P., "United Presbyterian" being too large a phrase for every-day use. An Englishman is above all things struck by the large place which the theological and ecclesiastical debates of the several Assemblies occupy in the newspapers. Discussions on difficult points of Biblical criticism, or on details of church polity and order, engross a space in the daily press which in London would rarely be accorded to anything but politics, art, or popular amusements. In the Assemblies themselves, the galleries are thronged by audiences content to listen for hours; dispersing late in the afternoon, only to resume their eager attendance in the evening. On one memorable day in 1876, I had the happiness to be present in the Free Church Assembly, when the Reformed Presbyterian Church, the representatives of the ancient Cameronians, was solemnly incorporated into the body, and there became to all intents and purposes one sect fewer in Protestant Christendom! The proceedings were partly formal,—the reading of documents, articles of arrgreement, etc., but there was a dignity and seriousness about the whole that kept the attention strained to the utmost. A vacant space had been reserved in the centre of the Assembly; and when the preliminary business was over, the representatives of the newly-admitted Church, who had assembled elsewhere to terminate, in their own Assembly, their denominational existence, entered in long procession,

COVENANTERS' MONUMENT, GREYFRIARS' CHURCHYARD.

HEAD OF 'WEST BOW, EDINBURGH.

and took their places, the multitude that crowded the hall standing in unbroken silence to receive them. It was not until the last had entered that the pent-up enthusiasm of the multitude welcoming their brethren found vent; and the proceedings of the morning were fitly crowned by an address from the Moderator of the happily absorbed community, which for dignity, tenderness, and real oratorical power seemed to me about the noblest speech I had ever heard. All this was but an episode. Now and then the atmosphere of the Assembly grows electric with the discussion of great religious questions, and of late years, as every one knows, these have had to do with very vital matters of Biblical criticism and interpretation, as well as with the doctrine of inspiration itself. The intense seriousness as well as the vigour and brilliancy with which the debates are conducted gives them a surpassing interest; the hearers in the galleries take sides, and are often loud in their expressions of approval or otherwise. The keenness with which all classes thus engage in religious discussion no doubt sometimes degenerates into acrimony; and the eagerness with which some points are debated appears to an Englishman out of proportion to their real importance; and yet on the whole the enthusiasm is healthy. Almost anything is better than religious indifference!

CRAIGCROOK CASTLE, RESIDENCE OF JEFFREY.

The associations of Edinburgh with literature, art, and science are in their way as signal and unique as its connection with matters theological and ecclesiastical. But this is a topic hardly within our present scope, or our Edinburgh "Pictures" might well include a portrait-gallery of men who have done more to influence thought and action during the past century than any equal number of persons taken from any single locality. Whether the title of "the Modern Athens" was first conferred in banter, or whether the chief reference was originally to the outward semblance of the city, with the Castle Rock for the Acropolis, we need not inquire. In sober seriousness, the intellectual pre-eminence of Edinburgh justifies the name. The very atmosphere of society in this favoured city seems charged with mental energy. For the scientific visitor there is the Museum of Science and Art, adjoining the University buildings, and admirably arranged, especially in the departments of Natural History and of British manufactures. The National Gallery of Antiquities, upon the Mound, contains a splendidly-arranged

45

series of objects, illustrating the history of civilisation in Scotland, from the flint axes and arrow-heads of a barbarous people, with relics from their caves and lake dwellings, down to the time when the ancient Celtic church had attained to a high degree of artistic refinement, as shown in ecclesiastical relics and sculptures of much beauty, and onward to quite modern times. There are some grim memorials, too, recalling times of strife and persecution : the " thumbikins " used to extort the secrets of the Covenanting recusants, and the " Maiden," that primitive guillotine beneath whose cruel knife so many of the best and bravest in Scotland fell. John Knox's pulpit from St. Giles's Church is also preserved in this great collection : with originals of the Covenants in their successive forms ; and—not the least noteworthy among the curiosities— the very " cutty stool " that Jenny Geddes hurled at the Dean's head in St. Giles's when he attempted to introduce the English Liturgy into the Scottish Church, on the 23rd of July, 1637. Close by is the National Gallery of Art, a noble collection which, if it were only in a foreign city, every visitor would make a point of seeing. Here also in the early spring is held the annual Exhibition of the Scottish Academy, generally, as might be expected, peculiarly rich in pictures of Scottish scenery, though with a fair number of other paintings, and often including masterpieces from the London Academy Exhibition of the preceding year.

KNOX'S PULPIT.

The visitor to Edinburgh who has time and inclination to inspect the interiors of great buildings must by all means visit two great churches, at least, in the city. The principal, St. Giles's, is often called the Cathedral ; though rigid Presbyterians disclaim the appellation, there being no *cathedra* or bishop's chair in their ecclesiastical arrangements. A mournful interest attaches now to the sumptuous and tasteful restoration of this building, which has for the first time brought out its full design, in stateliness of plan

QUEEN'S PARK, EDINBURGH: REVIEW OF SCOTTISH VOLUNTEERS, AUGUST 7, 1860.

and richness of decoration. The work was carried on at the expense of Mr. William Chambers, the elder of the two brothers who more than any other men have set their mark on the popular literature of the age, and the simple and graceful record of whose lives will probably outlast all the works that bear their name. *Chambers' Journal*, be it remembered, was before the *Penny Magazine*, which it has long outlived, both having been started in 1832 ; and the two for many years remained the chief helps in periodical literature to youths and working-men athirst for knowledge. Their one defect—and

CHOIR OF ST. GILES'S CATHEDRAL.

we must be honest enough to avow this—was that they were exclusively secular ; giving hardly so much as a glance at the deeper problems of existence, or at the principles of life and conduct which only religion supplies. The great saying of Dr. Arnold, now a commonplace, about treating common subjects in a Christian tone, expresses an aim which fifty years ago hardly existed. Nor did writers of the Chambers' and the old " Useful Knowledge" school ever recognise it. It was not that they were always insensible to the supreme claim of Christianity ; but they had deliberately chosen another line of popular instruction. And yet, that the last work of the veteran publisher and philanthropist should be given to a Christian church, which was solemnly re-dedicated to Divine service two days after his funeral, is a fact significant and beautiful. Earthly honours came just too late for him, and perhaps the memory of William and Robert Chambers will live more naturally and happily in the hearts of their fellow-citizens than if they had newly learned to call the elder brother and survivor " Sir William."

But I have been led too far from St. Giles's Church, especially as I wished to refer to another and a very different ecclesiastical structure in

Edinburgh as well worthy of a visit. This is St. Mary's Cathedral, erected for the worship of the Scottish Episcopal Church, and one of the most important works of the late Sir Gilbert Scott. It would be superfluous to attempt a description of this truly magnificent building: the first view of those who look for a masterpiece of architectural design may be a little disappointing, owing to the disproportionate heaviness of the spire; but on entering the interior the beauty and harmony of every part is felt at once, the general simplicity of plan being well set off by the elaborate magnificence of the details, especially in the choir. To pass in one morning from St. Giles's, the oldest of Edinburgh churches, to this of St. Mary's, the newest, is most interesting and impressive. More than six hundred years separate the two structures in point of date; and between the forms of faith which they severally represent, the difference has sometimes seemed correspondingly great. Happily, we live in days in which the true worshipper, however strong his preference may be for one or for the other, may find Christian fellowship in both. There may be many folds: but there is "one *flock*, and one Shepherd."

LEITH HARBOUR.

From these ecclesiastical reflections, however, into which we have been betrayed by our visits to these great churches, it is good to escape again into the open air, and, quitting St. Mary's Cathedral, by way of Melville Street, and passing by St. George's Church, and through Charlotte Square, to make our way, either by the stately houses and terraces which lie to the north of Princes Street, or by Princes Street itself, with its range of shops and hotels on one side, and its lovely gardens on the other, extending as far as the Scott Monument and the Waverley Bridge, and along Waterloo Place, to the Calton Hill. Here the visitor, if he feels so inclined, may ascend the Nelson Monument, which towers above the city like a gigantic telescope, and commands a magnificent view over the Firth of Forth in one direction, and beyond the city southward to the Pentland Hills. I do not know, however, that the prospect from the summit is so much finer than that from the base, as to repay the labour of climbing. Certainly, on a

VIEW FROM THE BURNS MONUMENT, CALTON HILL.

clear summer's day in early morning, before the smoke of the city, with that of Leith and Portobello, has obscured the scene, there can hardly be a more enchanting view than this from the Calton Hill, rich as it is in the beauty of both land and sea, while the "romantic town" as a foreground serves to enhance the charm. To the other monuments on the hill no doubt a passing glance will be given. Much cannot be said in their favour individually, yet in their combination they certainly add to the attractiveness of the place. The National Monument has the effect of a classic ruin; although, as every one knows, the picturesque incompleteness is due only to want of funds. Why the Parthenon should have been adopted as the most appropriate type for the commemoration of the Waterloo heroes, it is hard to say; nor why the monument to Burns, a little lower down, should also be classical in form. It was the taste of the times: and, to say the truth, the adoption of another style in the Wallace Monument near Stirling has not been so conspicuously successful as to make us altogether discontented with the classic ideal! In satisfying beauty of form, the Scott Monument remains unapproached. Still, the grouping of the somewhat heterogeneous structures on the Calton Hill is without doubt effective; and the large buildings on its southern edge, the High School and the Prison, are even imposing.

LINLITHGOW PALACE.

The railway journey from Edinburgh to Glasgow is not particularly interesting, save for the opportunity of visiting LINLITHGOW by the way, if the longer route be taken. The walls of the old Palace in their square massiveness are a striking object from the railway, and the traveller who has an hour or two to spare may well alight to explore the ruin, with the picturesque little lake on the border of which it stands.

> " Of all the palaces so fair,
>   Built for the royal dwelling,
> In Scotland, far beyond compare
>   Linlithgow is excelling;
> And in its park, in jovial June,
> How sweet the merry linnet's tune,
>
> How blithe the blackbird's lay !
> The wild buck bells from ferny brake,
> The coot dives merry on the lake,
> The saddest heart might pleasure take
>   To see all nature gay."

So sings the Minstrel, in *Marmion.* The fern-brakes are still there, the linnet carols as in the olden days, and there is enough of stateliness remaining in the shattered pile to show what the place must have been when the Lady Margaret, Queen of James the Fourth, there had her bower, in which, after the fatal day of Flodden, she mourned in widowed state. To Linlithgow James the Fifth conducted his bride Mary of Guise, who expressed her admiration of the place in words which are still remembered ; and here their ill-fated daughter Mary Stuart was born, in a room which is still pointed out. The church, dedicated to St. Michael, also deserves a visit, as " one of the few specimens still left of the ancient Scottish parish church." Part of it is still used for Divine worship. It was in

QUEEN MARGARET'S BOWER, LINLITHGOW.

this church that James the Fourth is said to have been warned by an apparition not to advance to Flodden : " Sir King, my mother hath sent me to desire thee not to pass at this time, whither thou art purposed : for if thou dost, thou wilt not fare well on thy journey, nor any that passeth with thee." It was in the street of Linlithgow, also, that the Regent Murray was shot by Hamilton of Bothwellhaugh, in revenge for a grievous wrong, for which, however, the Regent was not wholly responsible. Proceeding down this street, the visitor will notice one or two drinking fountains, one of which, dedicated to St. Michael, is surmounted by a rudely-carved representation of the archangel, with the inscription underneath, " 1720. SAINT MICHAEL IS KINDE TO STRANGERS."

A speedy run by Polmont Junction, leaving for the present the tempting

QUEEN MARGARET'S BOWER, LINLITHGOW (INTERIOR).

northerly route to Stirling and the Highlands, and past the great Carron Ironworks, brings the traveller to GLASGOW. Here he will hardly linger long, unless some errand of business or claim of friendship should detain him in the great, energetic, progressive, hospitable city; nor need we linger over the description. The broad and noble streets in the heart of the town, mostly intersecting one another at right angles, and the most important of them traversed ceaselessly by tramcars—among the best-appointed in the kingdom,—occupy a slope upwards from the north bank of the Clyde. The business streets are nearest the river; Argyle Street, continued by the Trongate, being the chief; farther upward the straight thoroughfares are lined with stately residences and offices, with many handsome churches, chiefly belonging to the three Presbyterian communities. To the north-east is the grand Cathedral, with its wonderful crypt. The windows of stained glass by which the cathedral is now adorned are modern, the finest of them having been executed at Munich. An hour or two may well be spent in the study of these very splendid specimens of modern skill, reproducing the style and tone of ancient art. The subjects of the windows are arranged in a kind of order, beginning with the Expulsion from Paradise, and continuing the Old Testament history along both sides of the nave; the choir and Lady chapel being devoted to the New. A catalogue, to be had in the building, gives a description of the pictures, with the

ST. MICHAEL'S WELL, LINLITHGOW.

names of donors, and of the persons to whose memory the windows are severally dedicated. The unsightly building near the cathedral on the south side is the Barony Church, once famous for the ministrations of Dr. Norman McLeod, and still greatly prosperous under the care of a worthy successor. Nearly opposite, on the site of the old Archbishop's Palace, is the Glasgow Royal Infirmary: and a little farther on, crossing a bridge, aptly named the Bridge of Sighs, we reach the Necropolis, a burial-ground notable, perhaps, beyond all other British cemeteries, for the number and variety of its monuments. The hillside on which they stand contributes greatly to their effect, when viewed from a little distance, and the column erected to the memory of Knox, towering in the midst of them, seems to give a fine completeness to the whole.

55

From the east to the west of the city, we may pass by the unpronounceable Sauchiehall Street, leading to Kelvin Grove Park, which rises steeply to the new University buildings. Few of our cities can boast a place of public resort at once so accessible, so beautifully laid out, and with so superb a prospect, reaching from the smoky city away to the verge of the Highlands. The University is a noble pile, worthy of a great nation; but it still awaits completion. The spire which is eventually to crown the tower will rise to a height of more than three hundred feet, and the whole structure, with its library, museum, and halls, will have cost about half a million sterling. The old University buildings are now turned into a railway station, it must be confessed with but indifferent success.

Pursuing our way westward across the Kelvin, by the Botanic Gardens, the wealth and tastefulness of the merchant princes of Glasgow show themselves in the long lines of sumptuous buildings with many a charming pleasaunce. The distant hills now rise to view. Few suburban drives are in their way more beautiful than that by the Great Western Road, through a pleasantly undulating wooded country, to the verge of the Kilpatrick Hills, where the Clyde is reached; and the way back is through the ancient village of Partick, older, it is said, than Glasgow itself. At some points along the route the river may be crossed by well-appointed ferries, giving access to what is really another city,—Glasgow south of the Clyde, extending from Govan and Pollokshields in the west to the crowded districts of Tradeston, Lauriestown, Hutchinsontown, and the Gorbals, with a nobly situated park, the "Queen's," on a height to the south. From this district, several handsome bridges lead back to the northern side, where to the east of the city the great open Glasgow Green will well repay a visit.

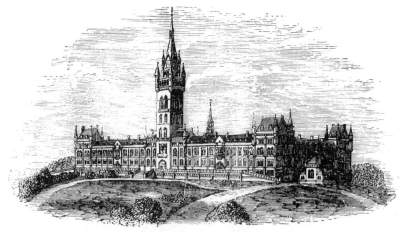

GLASGOW UNIVERSITY.

BY THE CLYDE,
TO THE WESTERN COAST.

ARRAN.

BY THE CLYDE, TO THE WESTERN COAST.

DUMBARTON ROCK.

For all Glasgow people the great holiday is down the Clyde. No city in Great Britain, perhaps none in Europe, has such immediate access to scenes where the highest beauty of land and sea combines with every bracing and exhilarating quality of the atmosphere to minister health and delight. Accordingly, "the coast," as it is familiarly called, is annually thronged by visitors, and the broad waters of the estuary are crowded by one of the finest fleets of river steamers in the world.

For several miles below Glasgow the river pursues a somewhat monotonous course between low banks, vast ranges of ship-building yards extending far beyond the city. The waters are muddy, and, it must be said, odoriferous, especially as churned by the paddles or the screw of some mighty steamer. Let no squeamish traveller arrange to leave Glasgow by a boat where breakfast is served between the city and Greenock. In truth, the fare is so good that it is a pity to spoil its relish by any intrusive accessories from the river! Many tourists prefer to save time and avoid discomfort by taking the rail to Greenock, or to Helensburgh, nearly opposite : but once, at any rate, the visitor who desires to have a full impression of what the commerce of this great city really is should embark at the Broomielaw, and note, as the steamer bears him swiftly down the stream, the enormous vessels, countless in number, and, as it would seem, from every nation under heaven, busily loading or unloading, or lying at anchor in the stream. We do not wish to trouble the reader with stating the tonnage

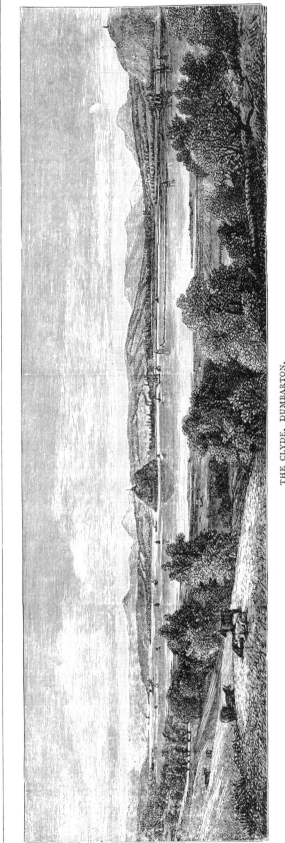

THE CLYDE, DUMBARTON.

that annually enters or leaves the port of Glasgow. These are found in all books of commercial statistics; and every one who has passed through those miles of shipping will easily understand that the amount is something enormous. But our errand to-day is one of recreation. After passing Dumbarton, with its singular two-peaked rock, the river widens out; we are in the blue water; and before Greenock or Helensburgh is reached the eye already revels in the splendid panorama of encircling hills, girdled by fair woods and studded with white villas, with misty mountain tops here and there beyond. A word must be given in passing to the steamers which ply along this favoured coast. They now form a fleet unequalled in swiftness and comfort, as well as in the lowness of their fares. At their head confessedly is the *Columba*, which runs daily between Glasgow and Ardrishaig on Loch Fyne, by way of Rothesay, and the Kyles of Bute. The *Iona*, which this magnificent vessel has succeeded, will be remembered by almost all Scottish tourists as having for many years performed the same service. For swiftness—the rate, I believe, is twenty miles an hour—and for commodiousness, these steamers are as unrivalled as is the scenery through which they daily carry their crowds of happy passengers. Other steamers, more fitted for a wild and open sea, ply throughout the year round the Mull of Cantyre; but we must now suppose the short holiday route to be taken. From Greenock for some distance the river seems at many points closed in by the hilly shores like a lake. Large creeks or sea lochs run inland upon the right, suggesting more exquisite beauties still of shore and mountain. Were there time it would be pleasant to sail by Helensburgh up the Gareloch, or, better still, to ascend Loch Long to Arrochar; whence again a short walk over a hilly pass would conduct to Tarbet, where the glories of Loch Lomond are full in view. But this cannot be for us to-day: we pass the pretty watering-places of Kilmun, Dunoon, Inellan, and others looking very lovely from the water, and all crowded with summer guests. We do not land at any of these places now: they are too hot and relaxing for us, although they have the glorious freshness of the sea, and their accessibility from Glasgow makes them favourite resorts of men of business with their families. On the left a more level shore faces the west, with the bracing seaside villages of Wemyss Bay, now accessible from Glasgow by railway, Skelmorlie and Largs. The Great and Little Cumbraes seem, in the distance, to bar the entrance to the river, and complete its lake-like appearance. But the steamer now crosses to Rothesay, on its lovely little bay in the Isle of Bute. There a multitude generally disembark; and truly, for a day's or a week's holiday, they could find no fairer resting-place. The wooded hills beyond the town are picturesque and attractive, and suggest many a pleasant little excursion over the heights or through the valleys of the island. Leaving Rothesay, the steamer enters the narrow passage between Bute and the mainland in a channel between green hills, strikingly beautiful in one or two places, especially where, near the entrance to a small sea loch (Loch Ridden), lies the village of Tighnabriuaich, which has only recently been discovered, as it were, by summer holiday-makers, but is rapidly becoming a crowded watering-place. We now turn sharply to the south, and soon emerge from the narrow Kyles into open water, with the peaks of Arran full in view. But our vessel to-day does not go near this island—which must be reached in other ways, but which should on no account be omitted by the lovers of bracing air and of noble scenery, especially if their pedestrian powers are good. Loch Ranza, Corrie, Brodick, Lamlash, Whiting Bay, have all their attractions; but Corrie or Brodick should be chosen by the stranger for his landing-place, as he *must* ascend Goat Fell. Every one will ask him if he did this: in fact, the question is so universal that, having failed in my first attempt, I found it advisable whenever I referred afterwards to having visited Arran, to add, "but I did *not* ascend Goat Fell." The ascent (2866 feet) is at once easy and most charming, in the two grand glens, up one or other of which the finest part of the route lies, Glen Sannox from Corrie, Glen Rosa from Brodick. We follow the burn nearly to its source, then turn off to a track amid vast rough boulders, very precipitous in parts and dangerous, if the prescribed path be left. When the summit is gained, the view over sea and land is on all sides

61

magnificent: and we no longer wonder at the question with which we were plied by our friends. Not to have ascended Goat Fell is to have missed one of the noblest and most varied prospects which Great Britain affords.

But Arran has attractions for others than mountain climbers. Its climate seems, if a flying visit gives sufficient warrant to speak of it, simply perfect—at least when it does not rain! The belt between the shore and the hills is so equable in temperature that the plants and shrubs of warm climates flourish there all the year round, while on every side breezy uplands are accessible. The glens, beside those just named, are rich in foliage as they approach the sea, stern and craggy in their upper reaches; the burns

LOCH RANZA.

that ripple over their rocky beds abound in trout and perch, generally small, but delicious. No doubt the accommodation and the fare are in general homely. At Brodrick the traveller may live sumptuously in a fine hotel, with prices corresponding: but in general the lodgings are the farm-houses of the island, quitted for the summer visitors by their occupants, who themselves make shift in cottage out-buildings. The houses are in great request, and themselves form a refreshing contrast with the arrange-ments and supposed necessities of city life. If any one wishes to prove with how little luxury he and his family can be contented, blithe and strong, let him apply early in the year—for this is necessary—to secure a farm lodging for July or August in the interior of Arran. It is not wonderful that many who have experienced this kind of life revisit the island year after year, hardly caring to go elsewhere, and often becoming very fanatics in their appreciation of this fair Atlantic isle.

But we must resume our sail in the *Columba*, now rapidly drawing to a close, as rounding Ardlamont Point, we turn our back on Arran, and the breadth of Loch Fyne opens before us. Calling at Tarbert, separated only by a narrow isthmus from the waters of the Atlantic, we sail rapidly past beautifully wooded shores into a little recess on the left, Loch Gilp, at the

GOAT FELL, FROM BRODICK BAY.

head of which the passengers stream forth upon the quay, many of them starting to walk across the neck of land that separates them from the Hebridean sea, others making their way over a dusty hillside to the canal steamer—it was the *Linnet* when we visited the place—and passing through some locks, rather tediously, to Crinan on the other side. Women and children selling milk and flowers greet us in our progress, pleasantly, but importunately. At last we reach the steamer for Oban, and perceive at once from the difference of its build that it is made for rougher seas than the holiday "swift" *Columba*, though still admirable in all its appointments. The course now lies past the once terrible whirlpool of Corryvrekan ("the cauldron of the haunted sea"), through a vast archipelago, the islands varying almost infinitely in form and extent. Sometimes they almost close around the ship, then again they open out grandly, disclosing the basaltic precipices of Mull to the north-west. The rocks on both sides now became grander, and give to the voyager who purposes to follow the coast line to the extreme north of Scotland a foretaste of what he may

OBAN.

expect. For soon the steamer enters a narrow sound between the green island of Kerrera and the mainland; a little bay opens to the right, and he is at OBAN, where the long range of shops and hotels fronting the shore, and the villas on the heights, with a mammoth Hydropathic Establishment, finished only as far as the first storey, not to mention the sound of the railway whistle, tell him that he has reached the great tourist centre, the "Charing Cross of Western Scotland." The charm of Oban to the stranger is that it affords so ready a way of access to all that is most beautiful in Scotland.

Yet a Sunday spent in the little town several years ago is not to be forgotten. It was a sacramental occasion. From an early hour boats were seen coming in from the surrounding islands, and at the time of service the little church on the hill was crowded to its uttermost capacity, while a larger congregation still had assembled on the green-sward without for a Gaelic service. The Highland folk had evidently come for a feast, and hour after hour they remained there beneath the blue sky, as one minister after another ascended the "pulpit of wood" which had been placed there for the purpose, and by turns expounded or prayed, or called the congregation to sing, all seated according to their wont; the Psalms being given out line by line. One of the tunes was the "plaintive *Martyrs*'," and never did those touching strains so much affect me as when the melody floated upwards in the still summer air from that congregation of hardy men and women. The sermon, part of which I heard, appeared amazingly to interest the audience, though no sign of emotion of any kind escaped them. They sat, in fixed attention, evidently prepared for any length of exhortation : but, a little wearied by the cadences of an unknown tongue, my companion and I went indoors and heard a discourse nearly two hours long, on the subject of *Solomon's palanquin.* "King Solomon made himself a chariot of the wood of Lebanon : he made the pillars thereof of silver, the bottom thereof of gold, the covering of it of purple : the midst thereof being paved with love, for the daughters of Jerusalem." Perhaps the singularity of the text riveted our attention ; it is certain that the sermon was not wearisome : its somewhat romantic tone seemed in unison with the place, and the preacher managed to bring out of his subject much good Gospel teaching, appropriate to the service that was to follow. Then came the "fencing of the tables," and the solemn administration, with further exhortation and appeal, the whole service having occupied more than four hours when we left, and found our Gaelic friends in the act of rising from their seats for the final benediction ; the solemnity of their attitude being instantly, and somewhat oddly exchanged for a scamper down the hills to their boats, while the delight of the dogs was unrestrained ! The evening sermon, to a much smaller audience, of course, carried us again into realms of imagination. "Who are these that fly as a cloud ?" was the text. The subject was almost like an enigma :—"Why is the Church like a cloud ?" I do not remember much of the answer, save that one point was the unity in diversity ; millions of drops making up the cloud, which

"moveth altogether if it move at all :"

wafted by the breath of the Spirit, and reflecting in its splendours the glory of the Sun of Righteousness. A magnificent sunset with a gorgeous environment of clouds seemed to point the preacher's glowing descriptions, which, whatever may be thought of their exegetical correctness, have ever since connected in at least one hearer's mind some refreshing and stimulating thoughts respecting the unity and glory of Christ's Church on earth with the summer splendours of the sky on that fair western coast.

We could not of course leave Oban without a visit to Staffa and Iona. Happily the day for the excursion was bright, the sea was calm, and we could enjoy to the full the little voyage that to some is a drawback to a visit which under any circumstances must be one of rare interest. As we approached Iona the first object visible was the ruined cathedral tower, surmounting the low dark line of coast. The sight brought to mind at once the ancient name and story of Icolmkill, the "Island of Columba's Church," with the Culdee traditions, from the dimness of which this fact at least

IONA.

emerges, that out of the churches in Ireland formed by Patrick's preaching there arose, a century and a half afterwards, an evangelist of princely blood,[1] who dedicated himself to the work of Christ in Scotland. As the old Latin rhyming verse has it:

> "Sancte Columba pater! quem fudit Hibernia mater,
> Quem Christi numen dedit Ecclesiæ fore lumen."

That the brave missionary and his companions chose this Hebridean island for their resting-place, was due to the opposition of the savage Picts; but they seem to have assiduously visited the mainland, and to have been

---

[1] See Usher, *Britannicarum Ecclesiarum Antiquitates*, c. xv. (Works, 1864, vol. vi. p. 230).

THE SHORE OF IONA.

successful in the highest sense. We can fully adopt the conclusion of Dr. Merle D'Aubigné, that though Columba might not have had the faith of a Paul or a John, he lived as in the sight of God. "He prayed and read, he wrote and taught, he preached and redeemed the time. With indefatigable activity, he went from house to house, and from kingdom to kingdom. The king of the Picts was converted, as were also many of his people; precious manuscripts were conveyed to Iona, a school of theology was founded there, in which the Word was studied; and many received through faith the salvation which is in Christ Jesus. Ere long a missionary spirit breathed over this ocean rock, so justly named 'the light of the western world.'

"The Judaical sacerdotalism which was beginning to extend in the Christian Church found no support in Iona. They had forms, but not to them did they look for life. It was the Holy Ghost, Columba maintained, that made a servant of God. When the youth of Caledonia assembled around their elders on these savage shores, or in their humble chapel, these ministers of the Lord would say to them; 'The Holy Scriptures are the only rule of faith . . . Throw aside all merit of works, and look for salvation to the grace of God alone . . . Beware of a religion which consists of outward observances: it is better to keep your heart pure before God than to abstain from meats . . . One alone is your head, Jesus Christ.'

"The sages of Iona knew nothing of transubstantiation, or of the withdrawal of the cup in the Lord's Supper, or of auricular confession, or of prayers to the dead, or tapers, or incense: they celebrated Easter on a different day from Rome; synodal assemblies regulated the affairs of the Church, and the papal supremacy was unknown. The sun of the gospel shone upon these wild and distant shores." [1]

Many a wild and foolish legend no doubt became attached to the later records of a life which we thus see dimly through the mist of centuries and the imagination of the great evangelist's biographers. We reject the Saint Columba of the hagiologies, but we are able to believe in Columba, the great simple-hearted missionary to the Highlands of Scotland; and if the form of truth that he introduced was defaced by some errors, there was at any rate the vitality in it which proved it to contain the essentials of the faith, and which in times to come was to accomplish its further purification.

The occasion of our visit proved of especial interest to the islanders, as it was the first excursion of the season. A large number came to the shore to greet our landing, and the conductor of our trip, in particular, having proved himself a warm friend to the islanders, in regard to their temporal and spiritual wants, was received with a warmth of welcome that it was good to

---

[1] *History of the Reformation*, vol. v. book xvii. ch. i. See also *Iona*, by the Rev. Dr. W. Lindsay Alexander (R. T. S. "monthly volume").

see. We visited the ruined cathedral, inspected the curious crosses which the island contains, and the unique burying-place, where in close array are ranged the tombstones of the old Scottish kings, forty-eight in number, it is said; Shakspeare's Macbeth being the last of the series, following his victim Duncan, whose body had been

> " carried to Colmekill,
> The sacred storehouse of his predecessors,
> And guardian of their bones."

From Iona we passed to Staffa, reversing what we believe is the usual excursion route. Here, too, the first visit of the season was hailed by the inhabitants; the sea-birds flew in thousands from the cliffs and caves, surrounding our boat with dissonant terrified screaming, until fragments of biscuit thrown abroad created a diversion, and prepared them afterwards to hail the approach of mankind! Had we brought guns with us, as many tourists do,

STAFFA; WITH THE " GIANT'S COLONNADE "

the effect might have been reversed! We entered Fingal's Cave without much difficulty by aid of some boats, which seemed to have been brought over in anticipation of our coming, and climbed the wonderful broken columns; our good conductor reaching the farthest verge, and when all the company had grouped themselves in the cavern side, leading off with the doxology, followed by a verse of *God save the Queen*. The effect of the strain, echoed from the vault of the cavern, and blending with the restless moan of the sea around the entrance, was something not to be forgotten, while the effect was enhanced by the wild cries of the birds, startled anew at this invasion of their haunts. After a climb by ladder to the summit of this wonderful island, and a walk on its grassy platform, we returned to Oban, with new zest for one yet further excursion northwards.

But now came in the difficulty of choice. Happily we have since had opportunities of enjoying by turn all the chief tours to which Oban opens

FINGAL'S CAVE.

the way, and they are all so rich in charm, that we hardly know how to counsel the intending traveller. He may take the steamer upwards, passing Dunolly and Dunstaffnage Castles, crossing the mouth of Loch Etive, and after a fine sail through the lower part of Loch Linnhe, halting at the point

FINGAL'S CAVE, FROM THE ENTRANCE.

where the white cottages and clumps of trees which mark Ballachulish and its quarries line the shore of a fine inlet opening among the mountains. Landing there, you are at the mouth of Glencoe; and a day may well be spent in exploring its gloomy grandeurs. A thunderstorm in the heart of this glen,

73

a few days after the visit to Staffa and Iona just recorded, was a wonderful experience. Only once or twice, in the Alps, have I heard such tremendous re-echoing peals, incessant flashes gleaming between, while a pair of eagles screaming overhead seemed to add to the wildness of the scene. The rain that followed came down as rain only can in the Western Highlands. In

FINGAL'S CAVE, FROM THE INTERIOR.

a very short time the burn in the valley had swollen to a torrent, and cascades were leaping from all the hills. This was a little beyond the scene of "the massacre," a tragedy on which enough has been written, and which no partizanship or special pleading can make to appear anything but an atrocious crime. The stern, frowning ruggedness of this great glen seems in harmony with the gloomy associations of its history, and well correspond with its name, which, like the Hebrew *Baca*, signifies "the Valley of Weeping."

Some travellers pursue their course up Glencoe over the dreary summit of the pass to Kingshouse, and thence up a tremendous ascent, followed by a descent through a vast treeless "Forest"—for in Scotland a forest does not by any means necessarily imply trees—to a little lake, then over a wild pass again to Tyndrum, near which the road is crossed by the

GLENCOE : THE ROAD.

Oban railway, of which more anon; and the route loses its character of wild sterility as it approaches the head of Loch Lomond. The journey is one which emphatically I do not recommend. For wearying monotony of savage stony grandeur, it stands out beyond any other day's excursion I remember; but this was before the days of the railway. A much finer finish to the drive from Ballachulish would be to turn westwards from Kingshouse, and to descend to Loch Etive, following the northern bank, and crossing the loch near its mouth, at Connel Ferry, opposite Dunstaffnage

Castle. This road leads between fine mountain masses all the way, with Ben Cruachan grandly towering to the south.

But, instead of turning aside at Ballachulish, the tourist may pursue his way up Loch Eil, into which Loch Linnhe suddenly narrows. Both sides are bounded by low hills descending to a level shore, where we now see the "crofts" or small homesteads with plots of land attached, of which so much has lately been heard. Some of these have a comfortable, well-to-do appearance as seen from the deck of the steamer, and contrast well with

GLENCOE: A "WILD DAY."

the heathery wastes above; while others seem hardly more than a part and parcel of the waste, forced by painful efforts into some semblance of fertility. The steamer touches at Ardgour, near the narrow entrance of the loch, where, on occasion of my last visit, the inhabitants of the village seemed all to have assembled on the pier to welcome a bright-looking lad, apparently of nineteen or twenty, with whom I had been chatting a little on board the steamer, who had been sent up from some cottage home to " Glasgow College," and was returning radiant with good humour from his first session.

76

It was good to see how he went from one to another, shaking hands with fishermen and peasants, and respectfully greeting the minister, who stood in the background of the animated group; then walking off rapidly with his mother and sister, raising his hat as he passed to the occupants of a carriage, evidently containing the great people of the village, who had driven down to the pier to show their interest in the youth's return. The whole scene, rapidly as it passed, was like some charming idyll, and was characteristic of one of the best sides of Scottish peasant life.

As the steamer pursues its way up the loch, Ben Nevis comes into view on the right hand, a vast elephantine mass, with none of the picturesque grandeur of outline which in some aspects it presents. After seeing the peaked Ben Cruachan, and the gracefully towering outline of Ben Lomond, it is hard to believe that this mountain surpasses both in height. Snow, it is said, lies here in drifts all the year round. When I was there once in April, the whole summit was covered with snow—some who had recently ascended the mountain telling me, to the depth of eighteen feet. The "swift steamers" had not yet begun to ply on these rough waters, the Caledonian Canal, which opens into the head of Loch Eil, was still closed, and Fort William was the end of the journey. The weather, however, was bright and genial, and the great Glen Nevis, which leads up to the heart of the mountain, was lovely with spring flowers and mosses in every crevice of its vast and rugged rocks, while the stream, swollen by the melting snow, dashed grandly downwards among the boulders. There was a charm in the place which summer visitors lose; and in a homelike little inn, exquisitely clean and comfortable, at the extremity of the village, one had leisure, denied in the full rush of the "tourist season," to dwell upon the aspect of the scene. Crossing the canal by a bridge near its outlet, I had a magnificent view of Ben Nevis, its snows and precipices lighted by the declining sun; and it was possible now to feel the grandeur of this monarch among Scottish mountains. With a very deep interest too, I heard, on returning to the inn, of those meteorological observations which have of late years made Ben Nevis so notable in a scientific point of view. Mr. Wragge himself was absent, but of course his work was familiar to many in the little town; and about the same time a singularly interesting sketch of his disinterested labours, from his own pen, had recently appeared in a scientific periodical.[1] For five months, from the first of June to the first of November, 1881, Ben Nevis had been ascended every morning by Mr. Wragge or his assistants, without one day's intermission; and the meteorological observations were reported daily in the London papers, for readers who could have but little notion of the toil involved in making them. The observations were first taken at five in the morning, at the Achintore

[1] *Nature* (Macmillan & Co.), March 22, 1883. I have to acknowledge the courtesy of the publishers in allowing the use of the following diagrams.

BEN NEVIS.

Station, Fort William.
The route then led
upwards for two miles and a quarter to
what Mr. Wragge called the "Peat
Moss Station," which was reached on horseback,
between half-past five and six. This point is but
forty feet above the sea level. There followed a
climb to "Livingston's Boulder Station," a mile and
a quarter farther, 840 feet high, reached at a quarter
past six. Another mile led to a lake, a thousand feet higher, on a small
plateau on the side of the mountain-spur *Meall an t'-Suidhe*, "The Hill of
Rest." Here also a station had been fixed, and observations were taken.

Soon after passing this point the pony which had carried our energetic observer thus far was left behind. Three stations succeeded, on the main slopes of Ben Nevis, at intervals of half a mile. Brown's Well, 2200 feet high, Red Burn Crossing, 2700 feet, and Buchan's Well, 3575 feet. This last was reached at half-past eight, A.M. Then came the final effort over

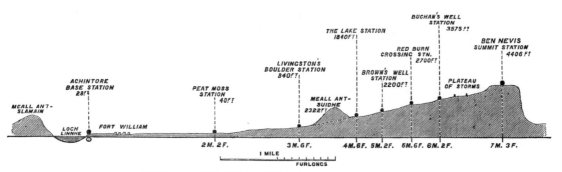

SECTION OF THE ASCENT, WITH THE SUCCESSIVE STATIONS.

rocks and boulders to the summit of the mountain, somewhat more than a mile farther on, 4406 feet above the sea, reached at nine o'clock. Here huts had been erected to contain the scientific instruments, and five sets of observations were made, at half-hour intervals, from 9 to 11, comprising the following elements : " Pressure, by mercurial barometer ; comparison pressure by aneroid ; temperature of air and evaporation (dry and wet bulbs) ; wind and force ; kind of cloud, amount, and velocities of strata ; hydrometeors and remarks in fullest detail as at the sea-level and intermediate stations at all the above times ; maximum and minimum shade temperature, solar maximum and terrestrial minimum temperature, and rainfall by four gauges at 9 A.M ; temperature of Wragge's Well and of ground at depths of 1 and 2 feet between 9 and 11 A.M. ; Ozone for periods

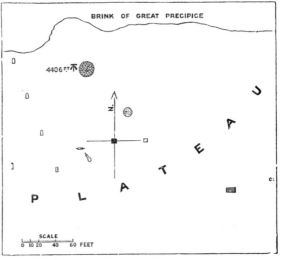

DIAGRAM OF THE SUMMIT, SHOWING THE POSITIONS OF THE HUTS AND INSTRUMENTS.

of $\frac{1}{2}$ hour, 1 hour, 1$\frac{1}{2}$ hours, and 2 hours between 9 and 11 A.M. ; also by two differently exposed tests for 24 hours ending 9 A.M. ; actinism of the sun's rays and of daylight by Dr. Angus Smith's apparatus for 24 hours ending 10.17 A.M. Hygrometric conditions prevailing about 9 o'clock the previous night by self-registering dry and wet bulbs, were noted at 10.50 A.M. Rainband by Browning's spectroscope was observed at various altitudes, and

79

its indications proved of considerable value. Full notes were taken of the cloud limits, and of any important changes observed between the stations."

The indefatigable observer then retraced his steps, making a second set of observations at each station, and reaching the foot of the hill by 3 P.M.; observations having been taken at the Achintore station simultaneously with every observation on the mountain side and summit, and being continued until night.

A few paragraphs from Mr. Wragge's account of his methods will be read with interest.

"I arrived at Fort William from Edinburgh on May 25, and at once proceeded to give effect to my plans. During the next few days I was

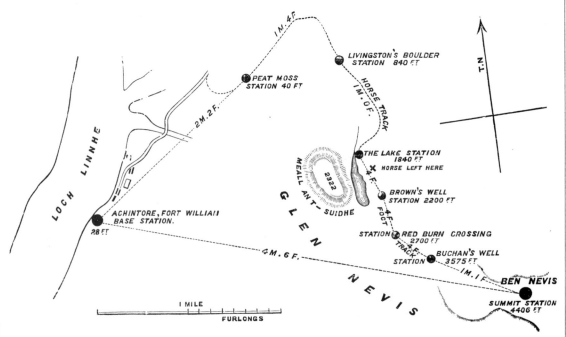

PLAN OF THE ROUTE UP THE MOUNTAIN.

engaged mainly in erecting Stephenson's thermometer-screens, and laying out the sea-level station; in establishing a new "midway" observatory at the lake, erecting screen, and building there a gigantic cairn for a barometer; and in reopening the temporary observatory on the summit of the mountain. It was only by dint of great exertion and a gang of men that I got all in order on the top of the Ben on May 31. I had no occasion, however, to alter the arrangements of the previous summer; and the heavy work of reopening chiefly consisted in digging out from the vast accumulations of snow the barometer cairn, hut, and thermometer cage which here, as a safeguard, incloses Stephenson's screen. The snow, in fact, was nearly four feet deep, and it was necessary to cut out wide areas around the instruments. I also erected another screen to contain Negretti and Zambra's self-registering clock-hygrometer, most kindly placed at my disposal by that eminent firm for the purpose of obtaining 9 P.M. values. I had also to fix a new roof of ship's canvas to the rude shanty that affords some little shelter from the piercing cold and storms. The barometer, a fine Fortin, had been left in its cairn built up during the past winter; and great labour was expended before the north side of the cairn was reopened, the stones being so hard frozen that a crowbar had to be employed. The instrument was found in good condition.

"Passing over all other details of arranging the stations and fixing

SUMMIT OF BEN NEVIS, FROM A PHOTOGRAPH.

instruments, I may say that I had all in order and commenced work on June 1.

"Of course my first business was to get the main observations—pressure, temperature, hygrometric conditions, wind, cloud, etc.—into full swing by June 1; and as I felt my way and got my hours and distances well under command I added to my work. Thus the ozone observing-system and the three extra rain-gauges on the summit were added on June 15, and the delicate operations for measuring the actinism of light on July 9. The additional gauges were established to discover if and to what extent the rainfall varies in the connection with the wind at different points of the plateau from the centre to the edge of the great precipice.

" During June, Stephenson's screens were in use only at the sea-level, lake, and summit; and hence at the other places the dry and wet bulbs had to be swung and the latter moistened afresh from adjacent water at each swinging. But aching wrists and sore fingers soon made me determine to have louvred screens at all the stations, and by July 1 they were in their places, and dry and wet bulbs, supplied by Hicks and Negretti and Zambra, fixed permanently in each. So above all was accuracy the better insured, and the whole system went like clockwork. I left Achintore before 5.30 A.M., and returned about 3 P.M., and the rate of ascending and descending was so regulated as to insure punctuality usually within a few seconds—often to the second—at the various stations.

" Two assistants, educated by Mr. Colin Livingston of Fort William—a sufficient guarantee for their ability—and trained by myself, helped in the work, and relieved me in the ascent of the mountain three times a week; and on these occasions I took the sea-level station. One of the greatest difficulties I had to contend with in the Ben Nevis routine was as to the pony on which I rode to and from the Lake, where it was left to graze and await my descent. Occasionally the stable-boy overslept, and I had to make up for lost time,—no easy matter, as the wretched track leads over deep ruts and treacherous swamps, and the poor brute had a trying time of it. Still more frequently the person to whom it belonged gave me rotten saddlery, in spite of all remonstrance; and on commencing the ascent the girth would break, and I had to turn the animal adrift and plod on to the Lake my fastest. This was decidedly hard, inasmuch as I was obliged to climb afoot some 2500 feet from the tarn in less than two hours by a circuitous route and over rough rock, stopping to observe at the other intermediate stations. Again, the pony often wandered in his hobbles, or having broken the tethering rope had made off to the moss; so also on the homeward journey I had sometimes to leave him and run my hardest over ruts and through swamps, by a short cut, to get my readings at the next station. Other trying parts of the work consisted in the journeys between Buchan's Well and the top in the allotted time, in having the two hours' exposure on the summit in bad weather, and in becoming chilled after profuse perspiration. The rude hut, with its walls full of holes of all shapes and angles, through which the wind whistles and the snow-drifts drive, afforded but a poor shelter from the drenching rain and cold, and it was impossible to keep anything dry. My hands often became so numbed and swollen, and my paper so saturated, that I had the utmost difficulty in handling keys, setting instruments, and entering my observations. Usually so laden was the air with moisture and so very dense and lasting was the cloud-fog that, even when no rain had actually fallen, all the fixings and instruments were dripping; and although, of course, I made a point of wiping the dry bulb, it almost immediately became wet again. Occasionally I timed the interval between wiping and fresh condensation on the bulb, and have found it wet again within *thirty seconds*.

"After November 1, then, I had to discontinue the work. The hut

HEBRIDEAN FISHER'S HUT.

had become choked with snow, and the carrying on of the undertaking satisfactorily impossible. I was, however, satisfied; and very pleased that I had secured five months' observations without the break of a single day."

The work is of national interest, and it is satisfactory to know that a properly appointed observatory is to be erected here, on the highest point of land in Great Britain, through the efforts of the Scottish Meteorological

Society. A series of observations so important ought hardly to be carried on in rude huts, exposed to the chances of weather, or of mischievous meddling.[1] Such well-sustained and disinterested enterprise in the cause of science merits the largest encouragement, although to reward it adequately would be difficult, if not impossible.

If the tourist should be disposed for an excursion in which every form of beautiful scenery, mountain, lake and glen, rich woodland and rippling stream, may be enjoyed in ever-varying combination, and where a fairly good road, out of the line of the crowd of travellers, opens up these attractions to easy access, let me recommend him to drive[2] or walk from Banavie, on the opposite side of the loch to Fort William, to Arisaig, on the Atlantic coast. The distance is about thirty-nine miles, the road for one-third of the way continuing along the shore of Loch Eil, which at Fort William makes an abrupt bend westward. At the foot of Glenfinnan, some six miles beyond the loch, there is a little inn, very welcome to pedestrians as a "half-way house." Here there is a colossal statue of Prince Charles, to mark the place where he first unfurled his standard in 1745, with a part of the clan Cameron, headed by the laird of Lochiel. Loch Shiel is now in view, grandly stretching in a south-westerly direction to the Atlantic. Leaving this, the road winds on in alternate ascents and descents, passing to the left a lovely little lake, and reaching the inn of Kinloch Aylort, ten miles from Arisaig. From this point every mile is full of beauty, especially when in the approach of autumn the hillsides put on all their splendour of colouring : while in all seasons, excepting those of incessant misty rain, the sea views are very fine. Arisaig is prettily situated on the head of an inlet, in face of a picturesque group of rocky islets, and just opposite the singular basaltic island of Eigg, with its almost flat-topped precipitous peak (Scuir Eigg), like a stupendous broken column, towering to a height of 1274 feet above the sea.

By timing the visit to Arisaig carefully, the tourist may catch the steamer southwards to Oban ; or northwards to Skye, Lewis, and Cape Wrath, should he wish to extend his journey to the grandest and wildest coast and island scenery in Great Britain. From Arisaig the steamer crosses the open sea, passing to the left the rocky islands of Rum and Muck, names to which the long ū's give a pronunciation more elegant than the appearance of the words ! Thence Loch Scavaig, on the southern side of Skye, is reached, magnificent in the lonely desolation of its broken cliffs of basalt and its rocky caves, though not without softer touches of foliage, shrubs and flowers, in

---

[1] I heard that on one occasion, before the instruments were so well protected as at present, a party of mountain climbers amused themselves with "shying" at them, ignorant, of course, of what they meant and why they were there !

[2] The mail-cart here, as in many other parts of the Highlands, is a really comfortable "trap," the driver of which is permitted to take three passengers at a reasonable charge ; although, of course, they must not have much luggage.

MARSCOW FROM SCUIR-NA-GILLEAN.

the ravines that descend from the Cuchullin (or Coolin) hills to the shore.

The description of this lake by Sir Walter Scott in the *Lord of the Isles* is well known, and is as accurate as it is poetical :

> " For rarely human eye has known
> A scene so stern as that dread lake,
>   With its dark ledge of barren stone.
> Seems that primeval earthquake's sway
> Hath rent a strange and shattered way
>   Through the rude bosom of the hill;
> And that each naked precipice,
> Sable ravine and dark abyss,
>   Tells of the outrage still.
> The wildest glen but this can show
> Some touch of Nature's genial glow :
> On high Ben More green mosses grow
> And heathbells bud in deep Glencoe,
>   And copse in Cruchan-Ben :
> But here—above, around, below,
>   On mountain or in glen,
> No tree nor shrub, nor plant nor flower,
> Nor aught of vegetative power,
>   The weary eye may ken :
> For all is rocks at random thrown,
> Black waves, bare crags, and banks of stone,
>   As if were here denied
> The summer sun, the spring's deep dew,
> That clothe with many a varied hue
>   The bleakest mountain side.
>   ·—*Canto* iii. 14.

Loch Coruisk is a little inland, and the passengers have often the opportunity, while the steamer waits, of climbing over rocky ground to take a rapid view of its melancholy grandeurs, as it lies there among vast and sterile rocks at the base of the pinnacled mountains. A long walk leads from the foot of Loch Coruisk through Glen Sligachan towards the inhabited part of the island. The path, which throughout is very wild, and in parts romantic, runs along the western flank of the Cuchullins, first climbing steeply upwards, with fine views of Loch Coruisk to the left, then skirting in its descent a little stream, beyond which the view of the peaked hills, and especially of Scuir-na-Gillean (the "scaur of the gillies," i.e., rock of the young men), is very fine. From the Sligachan Hotel there is a long uninteresting carriage road to Portree, the capital of Skye, which travellers who have kept to the steamer have reached more quickly than those who left the vessel at Loch Scavaig. The little town on its steep upward slope has few attractions, beyond the fact of its opening up to the visitor rock and mountain scenery of whose wild ruggedness nothing that he has yet seen could have given him an adequate idea. The drives inland are as well kept as with such a soil and climate could be expected; there are abundant facilities for hiring; guides offer themselves at every turn, and the signs of poverty and hard living everywhere prove that "the season" is an inestimable boon to the inhabitants. To the visitor who looks beyond the immediate enjoyment, and endeavours to estimate what must be the conditions of living all the year round, the very elements of the summer picturesqueness appear almost mournful. It was in the early spring that my latest visit was paid to these island coasts. The tourists had not begun to

LOCH CORUISK.

arrive, the swift steamers were still laid up in their winter moorings, and the chief passengers in the rest were commissioners and agents sent to inquire into the distress, and if possible to relieve it. One of the most frequent charges against the poor people—very pathetic, as I thought—was that they had cooked and eaten *seed potatoes* distributed to them with a view to the coming crop! A wicked thing, no doubt, but with starving children about them what were they to do? The questions arising out of all this sore need are plainly not yet settled. Immediate relief must be given, and the case of the Highland crofters generally has been so touchingly and strongly presented as to touch the sympathies of the nation: but what is to be the position of these honest hard-working peasants for the future?

THE QUIRAING, SKYE.

Here, too, is a "Land question," likely to employ our wisest thinkers and ablest administrators for many a day to come!

But our business is now with the picturesque. The excursion to Uig and Quiraing, with its fantastic table rock, will of course be taken; also, quite as interesting, though less strange in its surroundings, the drive to Dunvegan Castle, on the north-west of the island, the whole route affording magnificent views of mountain and sea. The Cuchullin hills are better seen from the road between Dunvegan and Sligachan than from any other part of the island; but to the nearer view of this wild romantic mountain range I am inclined to prefer such distant prospects as may be gained, for instance, from the heights above Strome Ferry, on the mainland opposite. On a

HUTS IN UIG, LEWIS, INHABITED 1859.

still summer's evening, nothing can be more beautiful than the view of the island beyond the narrow strait, with the bold and peaked range beyond, blue-grey and purple, dappled with cloud shadows and the gloom of many a ravine, standing out against the sunset sky.

From this wonderful island, the King of the Hebrides, the tourist may, if he will, pursue his way over a grandly open sea to Stornoway, the little capital of Lewis, or "the Lews." The charm of this voyage is chiefly that of the fresh and bracing air, with the changeful colouring of sea and sky. Lewis is bleak and wild enough, but after the wonders of Skye, few will care to explore this island or its neighbour Harris very closely. The sportsman and fisherman, however, will reap here a rich harvest. Another grand sea excursion is to Cape Wrath, the north-westerly extremity of Scotland, a magnificent granite headland chafed incessantly by an angry sea. The whole coast of Ross-shire and Sutherlandshire, indeed, from Strome Ferry to this promontory, is one succession of noble cliffs, indented by lochs and faced by innumerable islets; while, at almost half the distance, Loch Inver will be found one of those charming seaside nooks about which all who have ever explored their beauties prove enthusiastic. Sea, shore, river and lake, glen and mountain height, combine to make this little spot an earthly paradise. Would it were more accessible! The calls of the steamer here are infrequent, and the only other public conveyance, I believe, is the mail cart from Lairg, nearly fifty miles inland. But we must leave these

HUTS AT NESS, IN THE BUTT OF LEWIS.

fascinating scenes. None but those who have explored them can under-stand how great are their fascinations. Pure air, glorious scenery, the splendour of the sea and sky, and the pleasant if transitory companionship of the like-minded, who have also learned to love these islands and shores, deepen the attachment of visitors, who year by year desire no better holiday resort, and find that they can visit these scenes with increasing facility and comfort. There is no fear of a crowd to vulgarize these grand retreats. Only the few, comparatively speaking, will ever find their way thus far from the busy haunts of men. But these few will mostly be of those who have "eyes to see," and faculty to enjoy the wonders outspread before them. Many come hither in their own yachts; and the number of happy parties of friends who spend their summers thus is yearly

AN OPEN-AIR SERVICE IN SKYE.

increasing. For the many again, there are arrangements by which, on the payment of a moderate sum, those who desire to explore the western coasts may avail themselves, for a given period, a week or a fortnight, of any of the swift vessels that navigate these waters, passing if they will from one steamer to another, and remaining on board the whole time. They

CAPE WRATH.

need not thus plan out their holiday beforehand ; and almost wherever they may land to explore the surrounding country for a day or two, they will find another steamer ready to convey them where they will—weather permitting. This saving clause in the cruises of which we speak is of unusual importance. For, to confess the truth, these fair western isles, so lovely amid their grandeur in the summer sunlight, have their seasons of gloom and tempest, with long and trying days of driving rain and mist, with what to many will be worse, an angry raging sea. But even these have their compensations. The sunsets after storm are often gorgeous beyond a poet's dream; and the "mountain glory" is hardly to be apprehended by those who know nothing of the "mountain gloom," while the effect of both is aided beyond description by the changing aspects of the sea.

FUNERAL IN GLEN OUTIL, SKYE.

THROUGH THE WESTERN HIGHLANDS.

THROUGH THE TROSSACHS.

"THE DEEP TROSSACHS' WILDEST NOOK."

THROUGH THE WESTERN HIGHLANDS.

THE route by sea from Glasgow to Oban, described in the foregoing pages, has of late years found a formidable rival in the railway, which also gives to leisurely travellers a fine opportunity of visiting Loch Lomond, with Loch Katrine and the Trossachs. The "circular tour" to these scenes is indeed the best known excursion in Scotland, but it is too hurried for perfect enjoyment. If the reader who has not visited the country would like to know how in three or four days he can see as much as possible of its most characteristic and most beautiful scenery, I would recommend him to go from Glasgow to Oban by way of Loch Lomond, his halting-places being Tarbet, the foot of Loch Katrine, and perhaps Killin or Dalmally. A short run from Glasgow takes him to Balloch, where the Loch Lomond steamer is waiting for passengers at a little inlet, whence there is hardly a glimpse of the loveliness and grandeur beyond. It is well to begin such a tour quietly—it may be with a little disappointment. But the beauties of the lake soon unfold themselves, as the steamer swiftly makes its way among green wooded islands, and the mountain heights which line the upper reaches of the lake become visible in the distance. When the pretty village of Luss, on the western bank, is fairly past, the mountain grandeurs disclose themselves in ever-varying forms beyond the expanse of blue water at their feet. Ben Lomond towers on the right, while to the left the fantastic peaks of Ben Arthur, or the "Cobbler," and the grand precipices of Ben Voirlich stand out against the sky. There will be time, should the weather prove favourable, for the hardy pedestrian to land at Rowardennan, and to walk over the summit of Ben Lomond, descending at Inversnaid. The path is comparatively easy, and the prospect on a clear summer's evening is of transcendent beauty, ranging from Arran in the west to the Firth of Forth in the east. Travellers who decline this effort will nevertheless have from Tarbet, on the opposite shore, a magnificent view of the mountain, seeming to descend sheer into the waters to an unfathomable depth, and rising upwards to a noble pyramid. There is no place where a few days' summer quiet, or a Sabbath's rest, may be more exquisitely enjoyed. "I wonder," once exclaimed Dr. Chalmers, "whether there is a Loch Lomond in heaven!"

Across a narrow isthmus Loch Long is easily reached, or a long day's ramble may be taken in the wild and rugged Glencroe, at least as far as the "Rest and be thankful" seat to which Wordsworth's sonnet refers.

"Doubling and doubling with laborious walk,
Who that has gained at length the wished-for height,
This brief, this simple wayside call can slight,
And rest not thankful?"

"THE LAZY MIST HANGS FROM THE BROW OF THE HILL."

From this point it is time for us to return to Tarbet, and as soon as we can bring ourselves to leave its fascinations we cross to Inversnaid, made famous again by Wordsworth, in his *Highland Girl*. "The bay, the water-fall," of which the poet sings, are still there in unspoiled beauty: the "cabin small" has been replaced by a large hotel, chiefly known to tourists as the starting-point for Loch Katrine, which is reached by a five miles' drive or walk over a rough and uninteresting road that crosses one part of the watershed between the Clyde and the Forth. For the two lakes, so near, and to the thoughts of many persons so inseparable, belong to two different water systems. Loch Lomond, almost on the sea level, discharges its waters in the great western estuary. Loch Katrine, 350 feet higher, issues by Lochs Achray and Vennachar into the Teith, which joins the

Forth a little above Stirling, and so flows into the German Ocean. Such at least is the natural course of the Katrine waters: we all know how science and skill have interfered to turn a great portion of them westward also, and to make them tributary to human needs. Somewhat sneeringly I was told by a fellow traveller that we were going to see the great " Glasgow Reservoir "; and, in fact, knowing that the level of the lake had been raised four or five feet by embankment, with a view to this water supply, and that of course large engineering works had been constructed at the place of issue, it was natural to expect some diminution of the old romantic charm. But there is really little, if any. For one thing, the water-works are

LOCH KATRINE, WITH ELLEN'S ISLE.

placed at some distance from the more picturesque part of the lake, and are passed by the little steamer, on which we embarked at Stronachlacher pier, some time before we reach fair Ellen's Isle, the Silver Strand, or the opening to the Trossachs. The beauty that surrounds the outlet of the lake is thus left unimpaired. Then, the flow of water for Glasgow uses, vast as it is, bears but a small proportion to the capacity of the lake. Loch Katrine contains in round numbers 5620 millions of gallons: the daily supply required for Glasgow and its suburbs is at the rate of 54 gallons a head per day for a population of three quarters of a million ; something less than 40 millions of gallons in all.[1] Speaking roughly, therefore, the lake contains 140

[1] The average daily supply has been as follows :—

1871. 29,715,501 gallons.	1881. 39,144,907 gallons.
1876. 32,336,788 ,,	1882. 38,045,482 ,,

days' supply, were the rainfall entirely to cease and every tributary stream from the mountains around to be cut off. As it is, there is no deficiency, and though the trees on the margin of the lake seem in places to have suffered, the outfall to Loch Achray is, generally speaking, as copious as ever; while, to prevent any diminution in the river Teith, Loch Vennachar has been embanked, so as greatly to increase its storage; while little Loch Drunkie, a mountain tarn 416 feet above the sea, that discharges into Loch Vennachar (269 feet) is also used for storage.[1] There is thus no fear that the supply may prove insufficient; and in fact Loch Katrine at the very lowest falls but three feet below the old summer level, while, as we have seen, it may touch four feet above that level, a total range of but seven

THE SILVER STRAND, LOCH KATRINE.

feet. From the lake the water is conveyed to Glasgow, a distance of 34 miles; partly by tunnels through the hills, partly by aqueducts, overarched, and carried across valleys by lofty bridges, while in three valleys, those of the Dochray Water, the River Endrick, and the Blane Water, the water is conducted down the slope and ascends on the opposite side in cast-iron pipes four feet in diameter. Eight miles out of Glasgow, at Mugdock, there is a great service reservoir 317 feet above the sea-level,

[1] Here are the exact figures for the information of the curious :—*Loch Katrine*, raised 4 feet above the old summer level, has a water surface of 3,059 acres, and a capacity of 5,623,581,250 gallons; *Loch Vennachar*, raised 5 feet 9 inches, covering 1,025 acres, capacity 2,588,960,350 gallons; *Loch Drunkie*, raised 25 feet, covering 138 acres, capacity 773,750,063 gallons; total, 4,222 acres of water level, and a capacity of 8,986,291,663 gallons. These figures, and the facts given above, are taken from a remarkably interesting paper *On the Latest Additions to the Loch Katrine Water-works*, by Mr. James M. Gale, C.E., in the *Transactions of the Institution of Engineers and Shipbuilders in Scotland*, March 20, 1883.

with a capacity of 550 millions of gallons; and from this the water is carried to Glasgow by several mains, each to its own quarter of the city and suburbs. The result is that the inhabitants of this favoured town have everywhere in their houses and manufactories a practically unlimited supply of the purest water, carefully filtered in its course, and carrying health, cleanliness and comfort everywhere.[1]   Who that knows facts like these will not look on Loch Katrine with an interest even deeper than that inspired by the *Lady of the Lake?*   Or, at any rate, who will not be willing to turn his thoughts for a moment from the adventures of Fitzjames and Roderick Dhu to acknowledge that the most illustrious memory connected with this beautiful lake is that on the fourteenth of October, 1859, our gracious Queen, by opening the first sluice and letting the waters flow, conferred upon

one of the greatest cities of her empire this gift beyond all price ?

We have been led to dwell on this achievement of science somewhat dispro-portionately perhaps for a book like the present ; and yet it seemed not unneces-sary, to meet an impression not uncommon among those who have never seen Lochs Katrine, Vennachar and Achray, with their guardian mountains "huge Ben Venue" and " Ben Ledi's ridge in air." Nothing has impaired, and truly nothing can excel, the beauties of the

PASS OF BEAL-NAM-BO.

opening to the Trossachs as they unfold before the traveller, borne swiftly past Ellen's Isle, and stepping, full of expectancy and of Sir Walter Scott, upon the little landing near Airdcheanochrochan.   This portentous word, we believe, is Gaelic for "the high point at the end of the knoll."   He is now in the Trossachs, or the " bristly country ; " and perhaps his expectations have been

[1] The analysis of the water in one of the large mains during the year 1881–2, may interest our readers :—

ANALYSIS OF LOCH KATRINE WATER BY DR. E. J. MILLS, F.R.S.

Impurity.	Grains per gallon.	Impurity.	Grains per gallon.
Solid	2·1007	Nitric Nitrogen . .	0·0056
Organic Carbon . .	0·0980	Total combined Nitrogen .	0.0175
Organic Nitrogen . .	0·0119	Chlorine	0·4410
Ammonia . . .	0·0000		

unduly raised by the poet's description, for I have known some visitors to confess disappointment, and have even been confidentially asked, " But which *are* the Trossachs ? " The truth is, we pass through this lovely glen too quickly to take in all its beauties. We are in a hurry, perhaps, for luncheon at the hotel, or are wondering whether there will be room on the coach. It is best to linger. The crowd will soon have left; and when the distant horn announces the departure of the coach the lover of solitude may have his fill of delight as he makes his way to the Silver Strand, that edges the lake on the western side a little less than a mile from the landing, or rambles on the opposite side to the Pass of Beal-nam-bo (" Pass of the Cattle "), on the rocky flank of Ben Venue. The name speaks of the wild times when the cattle stolen by Highland Caterans from the pastures beyond were driven down this pass to the refuge of the Trossachs. *Katrine* itself, so melodious in its sound, is only this *Cateran* disguised! The Robber Lake! So at least Sir Walter Scott informs us. But, without endeavouring to settle this point of etymology, we can now re-enter the glen, in the light of the westering sun, and give ourselves up to the full beauty of the scene. On each side the crags, knolls, and mounds rise "confusedly," streaked grey, weather-stained, green with moss, purple with heather. From every crevice where a root could fasten spring the feathery birch-tree and the quivering aspen :—

> " Aloft, the ash and warrior oak
> Cast anchor in the rifted rock."

Look upwards at the sunlight glistening through the boughs, or downward on the long shadows that cross the path, or through the trees at the grey mountain forms dimly discernible. The view at every point is

> " So wondrous wild, the whole might seem
> The scenery of a fairy dream."

But even more beautiful is the quiet summer's morning in this exquisite glen, when the dew glistens on every spray, and the birds fill the air with music. The crowd of tourists will soon arrive, but at present the place is free. Walk or drive to Callander, by the Bridge of Turk and beautiful Vennachar ; you will soon meet the long procession of carriages and coaches, with red-coated drivers showing to their passengers the successive points of scenery described in the *Lady of the Lake*. " There "—pointing with his whip—" is Coilantogle Ford—now occupied by the sluice and salmon ladders connected with the water-works : " — then, breaking into poetry, the driver recites some lines of Scott. To him there is but one poem ; and every character in it is historical. It is pleasant to see such enthusiasm, even though after-thoughts of profit may be connected with it. We have driven through famous historic scenes beside some sullen coachman

BEN VENUE

IN GLEN DOCHART.

who had nothing but a gruff *Yes* or *No* to our most eager questions. Such drivers would find no place in the Trossachs!

Probably we may not be able to remain in the neighbourhood of Loch Vennachar, or there are lovely spots that would well repay the explorer. As a rule, however, these are as lonely all through the summer season as though the crowd of excursionists were not daily rushing past. One bright summer day stands out in memory, spent years ago with pleasant friends by "the only *Lake* in Scotland." For all the rest are lochs : this of Menteith, for some inscrutable reason, is always called a lake. Here is "Queen Mary's Bower" in Inch-ma-home, the "Island of Rest"; and here, with the "four Maries" as her attendants, the ill-fated princess passed her brief and happy childhood. For varied loveliness of woodland, streamlet, hill, lake, and island, with glimpses of sterner majesty beyond, no little excursion could well be more charming than this from Dullater, at the outlet of Vennachar, to the Port of Menteith and Aberford, whence, for the pedestrian, there is a grand walk over a lower spur of Ben Venue, past Loch Drunkie to Duncraggan, where the road to Callander is again joined. Callander itself, excepting the pretty fall of Bracklinn above the village, presents no points of special interest. The "Dreadnought" Hotel is familiar to tourists as a place for coming and going; but most travellers now seek the railway station; and if bound as we are now for Oban, they will soon find themselves on one of the finest routes by rail which these islands can boast. Many people complain that railways interfere with the enjoyment of scenery. In some localities this may be true. But here the natural features of the country are on so vast a scale that the little railway line (mostly single) and the infrequent trains seem no profanation either of the stillness or of the beauty. To the traveller almost every mile is now full of charm. First of all he proceeds up the glen of the Leny, a stream that flows over rocky banks from Loch Lubnaig to the Teith : the lake then opens up and the railway continues close upon its banks from end to end in view of crags and wooded knolls on the opposite side. Soon the line mounts upwards to a height above Loch Earn Head, a magnificent view of the loch with its girdling mountains being obtained from the railway carriage windows. Glen Ogle that follows is wild and rocky, the line being carried like a slender thread among its gigantic crags. At Killin Station, three or four miles from the village, there is a junction for Loch Tay, beyond which Ben Lawers rises grandly. Glen Dochart, which is next ascended, brings into view the mighty pyramid of Ben More, and the line still rises to Crianlarich, at the head of Glen Falloch, and to Tyndrum. After passing the summit level, we obtain a fine open view over Glen Orchy to the north, and soon after passing Dalmally reach the head of Loch Awe, near Kilchurn Castle. At Loch Awe Station a new hotel commands a grand prospect of lake and mountain, seen in too brief glimpses from the train, which after pursuing its way for somewhat more than a mile by the lake side plunges into the Pass of Brander, shared by the railway with the road and the

HEAD OF LOCH AWE AND KILCHURN CASTLE.

broad swift river. The latter is crossed just above Taynuilt, and Loch Etive is reached, near the outlet of which by Dunstaffnage Castle the train turns off through a green valley encircled by low rocky hills to its destination at OBAN.

The only other railway route to compare with this in varied beauty also crosses the Highlands from east to west, but is much further north. It may be entered at Inverness, though its proper starting-point is at Dingwall, where the line diverges westward from the railway to the north. From Oban to Inverness the best way is up what has been called the Great Glen of Scotland, by way of Loch Linnhe, the Caledonian Canal, Loch Lochy, and Loch Ness. This route has already been sketched in these pages, as far as Fort William : the part beyond, though the passing of the canal locks is tedious, is very beautiful in fine summer weather, especially between the green hills and woods that line the shore of Loch Ness. Foyers will of course be visited ; though it is far better to take a more leisurely survey of this grand waterfall, "out of all sight and sound," says Professor Wilson, "the finest in Great Britain," than is possible amid the rush of tourists while the steamer waits. It is a scene over which to linger through half a summer's day : and although the Lower Fall is by far the finer, the Upper is worth visiting too, and the paths up the glen are of rich and various beauty.

INVERNESS was to me unexpectedly attractive. I had read of a "little Highland town," but I found a modern city, bright, clean, and evidently prosperous, while the swift clear Ness flowing from the loch to the sea (quite independently of the outlet to the Caledonian Canal) added greatly to the charm. But there was no time to stay, beyond one quiet Sunday, where, in a church beside the Ness, I not only heard a most admirable sermon, but listened to some remarkably fine choral and congregational singing, without any instrumental accompaniment. If the service of song could always be so conducted, I thought, there would be no "organ question" to disturb the Assemblies and the churches! The next morning early found me on the way to Dingwall for what is called the "Skye Railway," having its terminus at Strome Ferry, in full view of that wonderful island. From Dingwall the first stage led to the broad open vale of Strathpeffer, with Ben Wyvis rising grandly to the north, while from the nearer foreground in every direction arose mountains exquisitely diversified in contour. The place invited a longer stay, even apart from the attractions of its mineral waters : but time forbade, and Auchnasheen farther on promised yet greater charms. After passing through a wonderful ravine and through many a rocky cutting, an expanse of rich pasture and lovely woods opened upon the view, with glimpses of a calm lake seeming to recede among the hills. The mountain heights that bounded the valley in all directions became softer and less rugged to the view, as well as almost infinitely varied in form. At Auchnasheen, on the margin also of a little lake, the railway was left awhile for an excursion

LOWER FALL OF FOYERS.

to Loch Maree and Gairloch, easily attainable by a good pedestrian, though in the season there is generally sufficient coach accommodation for the tourists who come so far. The route, however, is becoming better known, and certainly there are few excursions even in Scotland to compare with this for interest and grandeur. So much is now said about Loch Maree by those who have visited it that expectation is apt to be disappointed. Yet those who care most for the sterner aspects of nature, who delight in bold mountain forms, and see more beauty in the dark green of pine forests on grey hill slopes, than in the "birks of Aberfeldy" or the oaks and hazels of the Trossachs, will give the palm to Loch Maree over perhaps all other scenery in Scotland. The green islands on the lake are picturesquely beautiful, and Ben Slioch rears its head on the farther shore, a very giant among the surrounding mountains.

LOCH MAREE, WITH BEN SLIOCH.

A few miles farther, and the Gairloch is reached,—a noble bay, to the head of which a lovely valley opens, well named "Flowerdale." Hence, again, there is a sea route to the Isle of Skye or to Oban.

The traveller who has not left the train at Auchnasheen, or who returns to that station to pursue the westward route, soon reaches the summit of the line over a wild moorland region, then descends through a glen bordered by mountain forms of singular beauty until Loch Carron, one of the loveliest if not of the grandest sea lochs in the North of Scotland, opens out before him. For some miles the railway closely borders the shore, and in the summer sunshine nothing can exceed the effect of the purple hills across the deep blue waters. The view is seen in its perfection from Strome Ferry, the terminus of the railway, where the hotel is beautifully situated on a little eminence commanding the loch, the sound into which it opens, and the blue-grey Cuchullin Hills beyond. After all, I think there is no approach to Skye so fine as this.

Our two Western Highland Railway routes were now accomplished, forming with the Caledonian Canal and its connected lakes a vast irregular Z, from Callander at one extremity to Strome Ferry at the other, Oban and Inverness being at the two angles. To all travellers who can take but one Scottish tour we would say, let it be this. Only let us hope, again, that the weather may be fine. Auchnasheen, it is said, means in Gaelic, "The field of rain :" and the name is only too well deserved.

"LAND OF THE MOUNTAIN AND THE FLOOD."

THE CENTRAL HIGHLANDS:
STIRLING TO INVERNESS.

RELICS OF BIRNAM WOOD.

VIEW FROM STIRLING CASTLE.

THE CENTRAL HIGHLANDS: STIRLING TO INVERNESS.

THE Scottish Highlands are sometimes spoken of so as to convey the impression that there is a clearly defined mountain district, contrasted with "the Lowlands," as though the latter were a vast plain. There could hardly be a greater mistake. From Kirkcudbright to Caithness, there is hardly a county without its hill-ranges; and without leaving the Southern districts, the lover of mountain beauty will find noble heights and solitary glens, with many a rippling burn from tarns among the hills. At some of these we have already glanced; and it is almost with reluctance that we leave the rest for the grander, sterner hill country of the North.

It is at Stirling that the traveller from the South first begins to discern the immensity of the mountain region to which he is directing his way; and in comparison with the other routes that have been already described in these pages, or that may be sketched hereafter, possibly the region that lies about "the Highland Railway" affords the most varied as well as the wildest and most magnificent range of scenery. The line really starts from Perth, but the access from Stirling is an appropriate and striking introduction to its wonders, although it may be approached a little more directly from Edinburgh by crossing the Firth of Forth, and proceeding through Fifeshire. A détour by Dunfermline and Kinross I found very pleasant, especially as it gave the opportunity of visiting Loch Leven, famed for Queen Mary's romantic escape; but the journey on the whole proved rather tedious, and the route by Stirling seems preferable, especially if the traveller is imbued with

THE BORE STONE, BANNOCKBURN.

WINDINGS OF THE FORTH.

the romance of Scottish history, and is able to stop at BANNOCKBURN. The name had always a peculiar charm to me, perhaps through Sir Walter Scott's *Tales of a Grandfather*—surely the best "child's history" ever written: and although the place itself is flat and rather disenchanting, the very sight of it brings back some of the old enthusiasm. Standing by the "Bore Stone" where Bruce placed his banner—now protected by an iron grating—it is impossible not to recall that noblest of battle songs, "Scots, wha hae wi' Wallace bled;" or the stirring lines in which Scott describes the frenzy that fired the mixed multitude that watched the contest from afar :

> "Each heart had caught the patriot spark,
> Old man and stripling, priest and clerk,
> Bondsman and serf; even female hand
> Stretched to the hatchet or the brand.
>
> * * * *
>
> 'To us, as to our lords, are given
> A native earth, a promised heaven;
> To us, as to our lords, belongs
> The vengeance for our nation's wrongs;
> The choice, 'twixt death or freedom, warms
> Our breasts as theirs. To arms! to arms!'
> To arms they flew,—axe, club, or spear,—
> And mimic ensigns high they rear,
> And like a bannered host afar,
> Bear down on England's wearied war."

It is somewhat remarkable that in all the strifes of this period our English sympathies should be with the Scotch! The pride of the Scottish people themselves in their patriot heroes, no Act of Union or blending of interests seems ever able to diminish.

In Stirling itself the chief interest is concentrated in the Castle, which, as every one knows, surmounts a precipice fronting the plain of the Forth, the town being built upon the slopes behind. From the terraces of this grand rock the view is magnificent. Courteous guides will tell the visitor where Queen Mary stood to admire the prospect, or where Queen Victoria gazed upon the scene. Or, enticing you within, they will show the "Douglas room," and repeat the tradition of the murder foully wrought, pointing out also memorials of John Knox, side by side with relics from Bannockburn—a singular combination! Then for the sightseer there are the quaint decorations of the Palace, and the Chapel Royal, now a store-room. But the chief attraction is still without, in the glorious open plain girded by its amphitheatre of mountains. The windings of the Forth, partially seen from the Rock, so fertilise the vale as to have given rise to the saying,

> "The lairdship of the bonny Links of Forth
> Is better than an earldom in the north."

Appearing to rise almost sheer from the level in the distance, may be traced, in the west, the outlines of Ben Lomond, Ben Venue, Ben Ledi, Ben Voirlich, and of many lesser heights, while in the east the nearer and still more beautiful Ochill Hills close in the prospect.

STIRLING CASTLE.

The view is a fitting introduction to the mountain land. Of course we cast one stone, metaphorically, at the unfortunate Wallace Monument, erected in "the baronial style"—whatever that may be—upon a wooded crag nearly two miles off, an outlying spur of the Ochills that had formerly been one of the most charming features of the scene. We are told for our comfort that the structure is 220 feet high, and that if we please we can ascend it for the

WALLACE MONUMENT, STIRLING.

sake of the yet more extensive view from its summit. Declining the offer, and hardly caring to remain in Stirling, we pass on to rest for the night at the Bridge of Allan, a watering-place on the brow of the Airthrey range, luxuriantly wooded, and favoured not only by invigorating air, but by mineral waters, which on ascending to the pump-room before breakfast the next morning, we find we may drink *ad libitum*, on a small payment at entrance. Several persons are already pacing in front of the building with tumblers

DUNBLANE CATHEDRAL.

in their hands ; but the genial stimulating air of the hillside seems at present all we want, and a delightful ramble through the woods higher up sends us back to our comfortable hotel with appetite ready for a Scottish breakfast, to be followed by a long journey to the Grampian Highlands. The line to Perth crosses and recrosses the fair Allan Water, passing Dunblane with its old cathedral—worth a visit, were there time—then reaches Crieff Junction, or rather, the Junction for Crieff, that lovely resting-place in the strath or valley of the Earn being still at a considerable distance. Should there be time for a visit, an excursion up the wild Glen Turrit to the foot of Ben Chonzie would be found wonderfully enjoyable ; but we must now press on from the Junction, and leave these scenes for the time unvisited. Auchterarder is next passed, a name once famous in ecclesiastical controversy ; and the train traverses a broad fertile valley until it rolls into the wide echoing station of PERTH. The "fair city," however, need not detain us. Its far-famed Inches are broad level meadows. Kinnoul Hill is beautiful for its wooded walks and for its fine views towards the Grampian Mountains, while the Carse of Gowrie, an expanse of rich meadowland bordering the Tay, stretches eastward, and the blue waters of the estuary gleam beyond. It is said that Moncrieff Hill, on the other side of the river, is equally fine ; but I had no time to ascend both, or rather, as the time of my visit happened to be the Sabbath evening after the services of the day, it was more congenial to rest, in quiet talk with a friend, as together we watched the sunset over the distant hills.

Returning to the railway station in the morning, we find two sets of trains bound for the Highlands. One is by Forfar to Aberdeen and the east ; the

CARSE OF GOWRIE.

LARCHES AT DUNKELD.

other by Blair Athole more directly northward; both routes meeting again at Forres, and passing along the southern shore of the Moray Firth to Inverness. It is the Blair Athole line that is called distinctively the "Highland Railway"; and happy are those travellers who can linger at its successive points of interest, and explore at leisure the wonderful regions that lie eastward and westward, offering within a short distance scenes of alternate grandeur and loveliness, enhanced by the stern and rugged desolation by which, on the eastern side especially, they are shut in. At first, however, all is tranquil loveliness, as the train rapidly ascends the valley of the Tay, with many a view of the fair river. Dunkeld is soon reached—to many travellers the first introduction to the Highlands. The town is some distance from the station; and the best way to apprehend its beauty is to walk to

LOCH TURRIT.

the bridge over the Tay, from which a panorama of the richest beauty is obtained, the hills, nowhere vast, but picturesque in outline, being clothed to their summits with noble trees. The little town with its old cathedral tower is in front of the spectator; Birnam Hill, beyond the railway station, rises behind him. Undoubtedly at Dunkeld the two things to be done are to ascend this hill, and to walk through the Duke of Athole's grounds. Birnam is perfectly accessible, even to ordinary walkers; the "wood" which Shakspeare has made famous [1] is represented by some fine old trees; the path to the summit winds round a dense plantation of fir and birch; above which a grand view of the distant mountains is obtained, with Dunkeld in the foreground, guarded as it were by the wooded bluff of Craigie-Barns. The

[1] Mr. Pennant says that "Birnam Wood has never recovered the march which its ancestors made to Dunsinane."

sparkle of lakelets in the valley, and the luxuriance of the foliage on every height, afford a charming contrast in colour to the purple and grey of the mountains; while the broad and beautiful Tay may be traced both upwards and downwards for many a mile. It is only the background of rugged desolateness that seems wanting to the perfection of this fine view. The harsher features are softened by distance, and the spectator looks abroad as on an earthly Paradise.

Descending to Dunkeld, and visiting the cathedral or not, as his antiquarian tastes may incline him, the traveller must next make a point of visiting the Duke of Athole's grounds, passing on the way some old larch-trees, among the first introduced into Great Britain, having been brought from the Tyrol in 1738. There is a payment at the Duke's gates which nobody will grudge, and the prejudice with which some persons are apt to enter show-grounds of any kind will soon disappear. True, there is much of art in the laying out of walks and shrubberies, and opinions will differ as to the old effect produced in " Ossian's Hall," near the Hermitage, where the throwing open of a door suddenly disclosed a cataract which a cunning disposition of mirrors made to appear as though environing the spectator on all sides, and ready to pour on his head. He was expected to start back in fear, suddenly changed to admiration![1] This, however, was several years ago, when I last visited Dunkeld; not long afterwards I heard that some one,

[1] A naïvely amusing account of a visit to Ossian's Cave is given by an American traveller in 1835 :—

" On mounting a bank, I saw my guide at the door of a rustic temple, which he threw open on my approach, and introduced me to a circular mansion about 12 feet in diameter, neatly finished, and lighted in the top of the dome.

" 'This,' said he, 'is Ossian's Hall.' Then, pointing to a painting on the farther side, he began to explain :— ' That, as you see, is Ossian, singing to his two greyhounds and the maidens that stand before him.' I saw the listeners were alike enraptured, the dogs no less than the maids, and Ossian lost in the inspirations of his song. And while I myself began to sympathize with the group, and stood gazing on the venerable countenance, the heaven-directed eye, and flowing locks of the Bard, on a sudden, in the twinkling of an eye, by some invisible machinery, the painting was withdrawn—it was not to be found. The space occasioned by it opened into a splendid though small saloon, the farther end of which again opened directly on a cataract, 40 feet distant, and of 40 feet descent, which came foaming and rushing down the rocks, heightened in its powers by the full light of a blazing sun, and by the rocky bed and sides of the Braan, overhung by the thick-set trees, all stooping and bending to look upon the scene. It was grand and overpowering. My first emotions were those of a shock. The whole vision was thrown upon me so unexpectedly—the painting on which I was gazing had been withdrawn so miraculously, that I had almost fallen back on the floor with surprise. But the recovery into unqualified transport was as quick and irresistible as the emotions immediately preceding. It is an interesting device. The cataract itself, in its own natural forms, is worth seeing. It is made to spring upon you like a lion pouncing upon its prey. It seems actually to jump and leap towards you—and it takes a second long moment to be convinced that you are not lost, overwhelmed, and borne away.

" What gives additional, and partly a frightful interest to this scene, is a large reflecting mirror laid upon the ceiling above, which unavoidably attracts the gaze; and there you behold again the entire flood, with all its terrors impending, and it seems impossible to escape it. It is a most imposing spectacle.

" 'Walk in, walk in,' said my guide, stepping himself before me into the saloon, as if to convince me it was safe notwithstanding, as he saw me wrapt in amazement. I followed, and behold ! I saw myself thrown full length from the walls on the right and left, presenting my front and rear, and both my sides, with every form and shape I wore, from every point of the compass. I turned, and saw myself turning into a thousand shapes. I looked up, and there saw myself looking down upon myself, and standing on my feet against the heavens. I moved onward, and whichever way I went, saw myself moving in various directions—in one place slowly, in another quickly, in another quicker still, and in another darting forward at a fearful rate. He that has not philosophy enough to find out this secret, may ask me another time."—*Four Years in Great Britain*, by Calvin Colton.

whose æsthetics probably were too much for his honesty, had blown up the place with gunpowder, and left the falls to produce their own impression. Whether Ossian's Hall has been rebuilt I do not know. But, apart from such devices, the natural beauties of the scene are of such a kind as to be really enhanced by taste and culture. The Tay, with its lovely tributary the Braan, the surrounding hills, and the kindly soil, were all ready to hand; and the result of wisely directed expenditure and labour is seen in

HERMITAGE BRIDGE.

the charm of the turfy walks, the magnificence of the innumerable trees, and the selection of best points for the opening up of vistas, whence the chief beauties of the place may be seen. The Hermitage bridge and fall in the Braan Valley is perhaps the place that will most tempt the lingering footsteps of the visitor; although the "Rumbling Bridge" beyond (not to be confounded with the more celebrated Rumbling Bridge over the Devon, between Kinross and Stirling) is romantically wild. Altogether, it will be seen, Dunkeld is a place that may well become the Capua of the tourist who gives way to its fascinations. There is harder work before him, if he wishes to see the Highlands as they are. For, as we proceed northwards, we shall leave this luxuriance and splendour behind, and shall better perhaps be able to enter into the description of Dr. Beattie, author of *The Minstrel*, and of *Essays on Taste*, who thus refers to the Scottish Highlands:

"The Highlands of Scotland are a picturesque but in general a melancholy country. Long tracts of mountainous desert, covered with dark heath, and often obscured by misty weather; narrow valleys, thinly inhabited, and bounded by precipices resounding with the fall of torrents; a soil so rugged and a climate so dreary as in many parts to admit neither the amusements of pasturage nor the labours of agriculture; the mournful dashing of waves along the friths and lakes that intersect the country; the portentous noises which every change of the wind and every increase and diminution of the waters is apt to raise in a lonely region, full of echoes, and rocks, and caverns; the grotesque and ghastly appearance of such a landscape by the light of the moon —objects like these diffuse a gloom over the fancy, which may be compatible enough with occasional and social merriment, but cannot fail to tincture the thoughts of a native in the hour of silence and solitude."

Dr. Beattie's remarks occur in an *Essay on Music*, and are intended to explain how the Highland music is naturally plaintive and much in minor key; but that it is not therefore devoid of pleasing melody, the works of great composers, notably Mendelssohn in his "Highland Symphony," as well as the native Scottish music, sufficiently attest. Yet the description has interest, as showing how much the enthusiasm about Highland scenery is the result of association. That the taste for such scenery is of comparatively recent origin is shown in the *Letters* of the poet Gray, who writes almost as if the wonder and beauty of the Highlands were a new discovery. It must be remembered that General Wade's roads, giving easy access for the first time to the chief beauties of this mountain district, were but newly opened. "The Lowlands," writes Gray, "are worth seeing once, but the mountains are ecstatic, and ought to be visited in pilgrimage once a year." And again, speaking of Killiecrankie, "A hill rises, covered with oak, with grotesque masses of rock staring from among their trunks, like the sullen countenance of Fingal and all his family, frowning on the little mortals of modern days. From between this hill and the adjacent mountains, pent in a narrow channel, comes roaring out the river Tummel, and falls headlong down, enclosed in white foam, which rises in a mist all around it. But my paper is deficient, and I must say nothing of the Pass itself, the black river Garry, the Blair of Athol, Mount Beni-gloe, my return (by another road) to Dunkeld, the Hermitage, the *Stra-Brann*, and the Rumbling Brigg. In short, since I saw the Alps, I have seen nothing sublime till now." [1]

The railway, keeping for the most part to the valley, shuts out at present the sterner features of the scenery; though by-and-by it will pass

---

[1] See Gray's *Letters to the Rev. W. Mason*, 1765, p. 348, and *Letter to Dr. Wharton* (*Works*, Pickering), vol. iv. p. 61.

through a dreary country enough! The route continues from Dunkeld to the point where, in an open valley, the Tay branches to the west: the river that comes down from the north to join it at this spot is the Tummel. It is worth while again to leave the direct line for a brief visit to Aberfeldy with its "birks," or birch-trees, and pretty waterfall. As far as this point there is now a branch railway, so that the visit can be made with but small expenditure of time, although the leisurely traveller will find the drive or walk by the river past Taymouth Castle and as far

BIRKS OF ABERFELDY.

as Kenmore very lovely. Here Loch Tay opens up amid a scene of perfect sylvan beauty, with Ben Lawers, the sixth[1] highest mountain in Scotland, 3984 feet in height, rising grandly to the north, and the purple hills about Killin at the head of the loch, ten miles distant, affording some hint of the

---

[1] Which are the first five? We take the list from Mr. Baddeley's *Guide to the Highlands*: Ben Nevis, 4406 feet; Ben Muich Dhui, 4296; Braeriach, 4248; Cairn Toul, 4241; Cairngorm, 4084. These last four form one stupendous irregular quadrangle about the source of the Dee. Ben Lomond comes only twenty-fourth, with a height of 3192 feet. There are no fewer than *forty* summits, from Ben Nevis to Ben Venue (2393 feet), that may rank as mountains of the first class.

sterner grandeurs in the west. At Killin, as shown in a previous chapter, the railway to Oban may be joined : but our present purpose is to return to the northward route. The Tummel, whose course the railway now ascends as far as Pitlochrie, has been called the "loveliest river in Scotland;" but its chief beauties will be seen by those who have time to turn off from Pitlochrie up to Lochs Tummel and Rannoch. The combinations of wood and rock almost along the whole route are exquisite, and the Falls of the Tummel, though not high, are striking when the river is in full flood. I ferried across at the foot of the former lake to a point where a rock, easily reached, commands a superb view, known as "the Queen's," over the loch with its surrounding mountains, clothed along their bases with noble woods, their endless curves and slopes culminating in the mighty pyramid of Schiehallion. Should it be impossible to proceed as far as Loch Rannoch, the visitor may well turn back to Pitlochrie. He will see nothing finer of its kind in all Scotland. The Hydropathic Establishment at Pitlochrie attracts many visitors : the vale here expands into a wide strath ; the air, without being chill or harsh, is very bracing, and, though I cannot here speak from experience, it is said to be well adapted for tender lungs in winter, being dry and pure, while all the sunshine that there is, falls upon this happy sheltered valley.

Instead of resuming the railway journey at Pitlochrie, the traveller should—I might almost say *must*, for the sake of the rich beauty of the scene, proceed on foot or by carriage along the road as far as Killiecrankie, passing up the river Garry from its junction with the Tummel. Road, rail, and river, are all carried along the glen, and though even the railroad does not spoil its magnificence, but, on the contrary, affords many fine views of the wooded heights which seem to close it in, the best view, incomparably, is from the path below, close by the rushing river. A chatty, and, as he described himself, a *vara ceevil*, guide accompanied us : such attendance seems to be the rule when the footpath is taken. He was, as Scottish guides generally are, full of honest enthusiasm for the beautiful ravine of which he was the custodian. The only defect of the pass is that there is so little of it. Not far from the end, we reach the Soldier's Leap, the river being hemmed in by great boulders to a width of not more than ten or twelve feet, where it is said a Highland soldier, hotly pursued after the battle in July 1689, cleared the chasm and saved his life. There always is a Lover's Leap, a Soldier's Leap, or a Smuggler's Leap, over such narrow gorges! The battle-field is just outside the glen, not far from the station, and close by Urrard House, where Claverhouse died from the wound received in the conflict.

We seem to linger on these fair scenes : but in fact we are not yet at an hour's distance by train from Dunkeld. Yet a little higher, and we reach Blair Athole, where now the traveller begins to feel the coldness of the hills. The village lies in an open plain, and possesses no remarkable

GLEN TILT.

features, apart from the castle and grounds of " the Duke." These I did not care much to see, nor even to visit the grave of Claverhouse, who is interred here, but without a monument. For time was limited ; and Glen Tilt, that wondrous path into the mountain land, had supreme attractions. The Tilt is the little river which here comes down from the east into the Garry ; and

BRUAR WATER.

after following its upward course through a beautiful valley for a few miles, we emerge upon a grand bare glen, in the bed of which the stream dashes among its rocks. A narrow path is carried along the mountain side on the right bank of the river : opposite and in front of the pedestrian, hills rise beyond hills, in endless variety of bold magnificent outline ; torrents, which in dry weather dwindle into rivulets, descend from the heights; and one of these, the Tarff, when in flood has proved a barrier to many a stout pedestrian. Readers of the *Journal of our Life in the Highlands* will remember a picture of the royal party crossing the ford on horseback. This seems adventurous enough; but sometimes the ford has been entirely impracticable, and the traveller on foot who has been resolved to proceed has found it necessary to ascend the rough and broken path by the torrent for about two miles, to some rude stepping-stones. Life has even been lost at the ford; but quite recently a bridge has been placed over the stream. Some distance higher up the pass, the Tilt, now an inconsiderable burn, is easily crossed; Loch Tilt, the desolate mountain tarn from which it issues, is a little to the left; and the weary traveller, having gained the summit, is at the watershed between the systems of the Tay and the Dee, on the border of the counties Perth and Aberdeen. Before him are the giants of the Grampians, Cairntoul, Ben-Muich-dhui, and Cairngorm; and the stream which begins to appear through the stones and heather on his right hand is one of the affluents of the Dee. He is now on his way to Braemar; but we cannot follow him, as we must return to complete our journey over the "Highland line."

After leaving Blair Athole, this line becomes very dreary; the last of the woodland glens, with whose beauty we have been almost surfeited, being at the Falls of the Bruar, a tributary of the Garry, to the right. The trains mostly stop at Struan Station, and I would strongly recommend any tourist who cares to see another cataract to alight there and walk up to the series of falls. In its higher reaches the torrent dashes over the wildest, grimmest rocks; lower down the ravine is clothed with firs and other trees, in accordance with the petition of Burns, who in his admiration of the scene felt that it only needed the adornment of woodland:

> "Let lofty firs and ashes cool
>   My lowly banks o'erspread,
> And view, deep-bending in the pool,
>   Their shadows' watery bed.
> Let fragrant birks, in woodbines drest,
>   My craggy cliffs adorn;
> And for the little songster's nest,
>   The close embowering thorn."

The line now borders the Forest of Athole—a vast dreary undulating waste, scarred by many a storm, with boulders from the heights lying in all directions, to tell of fierce battling of the elements through winter days and nights. The Garry to the right flows over its wild, rocky, treeless bed; few habitations of men appear, and the glories of the distant hills are mostly hidden by the high curves of the desert region close at hand. This is the district of which we of the south so often read in winter time that it is "snowed up," "impassable." More than once, a train has been

LOCH RUICHT AND CAIRNGORM.

actually missing, until dug out—as wanderers on the St. Bernard are discovered by the faithful hounds! In summer time, however, the air is
exhilarating, and some indefatigable travellers who have climbed on foot
this watershed between the Tay and the Spey have assured me that they
found Glengarry delightful to the end. Near the summit of the line the
river is crossed; Loch Garry, from which it issues, lies a little to the left:
and at the Pass of Drumouchter ("the upper ridge") a "dip" between the
counties of Perth and Inverness, the highest point is reached, fifteen hundred
feet above the sea-level, near two singular mountains, the "Badenoch Boar"
and the "Athole Sow," which rise right and left of the line, while a little
farther on is a glimpse of Loch Ericht—the Scottish Wastwater, only
gloomier and bigger. The running stream which we now cross and recross
in its stony bed, shows us that we are beginning to descend; and the pace
quickens through the dreary wilderness until we reach the Spey, already a
fine river swiftly flowing from the west; and fair woods and pasture land
are once more seen. Kingussie (of which the ū, be it observed, is long) is
the first considerable village reached; the line soon skirts a pretty little
lake (Loch Inch), and beyond the woods on our right hand the highest
mountains of the Grampian range appear; not frowningly as seen from
Glen Tilt, but with considerable beauty of outline, enhanced by the foreground of forest. Rothiemurchus, on Spey-side, is a most attractive resting-
place, as I can testify, from the memory of bright summer days spent in
roaming through the forests, or climbing the neighbouring heights, or
pleasant converse with friends in a certain shooting-lodge not far from the
mighty slopes and ravines of Cairngorm. For we are now in the haunts
of the wild deer; and the sport which to its votaries not unnaturally seems
the noblest and most inspiriting, as well as the most healthful form of
recreation, engrosses the thoughts of all. It is indeed difficult not to share
the enthusiasm of the deerstalker, when some noble quarry—the prize of skill,
patience, and hardy endurance—is brought home in triumph from the hills.
Grouse-shooting, too, though making a far inferior claim upon the physical
powers, has its ardent votaries, and a glance down the pages of the *Sportsman's Guide to the Rivers, Lochs, Moors, and Deer Forests of Scotland*, published monthly in the summer, will show by the rents attached to the several
"shootings," how highly the opportunity of sport is rated. Still the sport
is but secondary, and the main gift of these wild moors and mountain airs
is equally for those who have never held a gun. It is the gift of health,
recovered energy of brain and limb, elasticity of spirits, power to resolve
and to achieve, so that much of the noblest work wrought by our highest
and best through the winter and the spring, may be traced to those
autumnal days spent among the moors of Scotland.

The Spey now gathers volume, and the railroad continues close beside
it as far as Grantown; the views of the river, the woodland and the distant

hills continuing very fine, notably where the Braes of Abernethy mark the confluence of the little river Nethy from the east with the grander stream. A beautiful excursion of about ten miles may be taken from Grantown to Loch Ruicht, near Glen More, reflecting on its surface the precipitous sides of Cairngorm and the summits of the greater and smaller Bynach. The scenery around is of the wildest character—the neighbouring moor is studded with pine trunks blackened by fire; the forest is said, and I believe unjustly, to have been maliciously set on fire, and the crime is spoken of as the "Shepherd's Revenge."

The loch at its western extremity is the resort of wild fowl, who breed without disturbance among the water-lilies and flags. At the other end the sandy beach is indented with the countless footprints of the deer, who come down to drink, or to relieve themselves from flies, by swimming to the opposite shore. To the east of the loch, lies a rocky defile known as "The Thieves' Road," along which the cattle "lifted" from their southern neighbours were driven by the Highland marauders. The mountains become less elevated; Strathspey opens to the right, and there is a pleasant route along the banks of the river, turning off some miles below its mouth in the direction of ELGIN. Here there is little to be seen but the cathedral, once a truly noble pile, and now imposing in its ruins. The western towers, though dilapidated, stand in their original massiveness: and the chapter-house at the north-east angle is almost intact;—"an elegant octagonal room supported by one slender central pillar beautifully flowered and clustered, which sends forth tree-like as it approaches the roof its branches to the different angles, each with its peculiar incrustation of rich decorations, and its grotesque corbel." The desk to which a copy of the Scriptures was formerly chained is still attached to the pillar. The architecture of the cathedral is in general "Decorated English;" the building was founded in 1224, burned in 1390 by Alexander Stewart, son of Robert II., commonly called the Wolf of Badenoch, and rebuilt during the first quarter of the fifteenth century. A magnificent steeple rose from the centre, but this fell in 1506, and being rebuilt to the height of 198 feet, fell again in 1711. Before this the building had been irretrievably despoiled in 1568 by the Regent Murray, who sold its leaden roof for money to pay his soldiers.

Perhaps, however, some of the most interesting of the reminiscences connected with this venerable pile are those connected with the name of Andrew Anderson. A little dark room is still shown to the visitor between the chapter-house and the north cloister, said to have been anciently used as a lavatory, or, according to some, as the sacristy of the building. Here, about the year 1747, a poor distraught woman took up her abode, with an infant, whom she cradled in an ancient font. Once Margaret Gilzean had been among the loveliest of the fair maidens of Elgin; but she had married

THE GRAMPIANS
AS SEEN FROM AVIEMORE.

ROTHIEMURCHUS FOREST IN THE MIDDLE
DISTANCE.

a soldier, and had gone off with him without her parents' consent; he seems
to have fallen in one of the battles of the '45 rebellion, and the poor young
widow with her babe returned to find herself despised and disowned.
Under the accumulated trouble her wits gave way, and resisting all tardy
offers of kindness and shelter, she clung to this forlorn home in the ruined
cathedral, wandering about with her boy, living on charity, and known by
all as "daft Mary Gilzean, a harmless creature, that wept and sang by

ELGIN CATHEDRAL.

turns." The boy Andrew received a gratuitous education at the Elgin
Grammar School, being appointed "Pauper" to that institution, sweeping the
rooms and tending the fires in return for the instruction received. At
the end of his school course he was apprenticed to a cruel master, a stay-
maker by trade—brother to the soldier Anderson, his father—from whose harsh
treatment at last he absconded and found his way to London. He obtained
work as a tailor's assistant, and in that capacity attracted the notice of an

officer bound for India, who was struck by his appearance and induced him to enlist as his servant.

Some forty or forty-five years afterwards Andrew Anderson returned, after many an adventure that it would take too long to tell, a Lieutenant-General in the East India Company's service. None recognised him, as he sought the

ON THE FINDHORN.

cathedral which had so strangely sheltered his infancy, and inquired of the old sexton, Saunders Cooke, "if he knew whereabouts in the churchyard a poor woman called Marjory Gilzean had been buried." "Na," answered Saunders, "she was a puir worthless craitur; naebody kens where she is buried. But I can tell ye where she lived. It was in that place they ca' the Sacristy.

VIEW FROM THE LADIES' WALK, GRANTOWN, SPEYSIDE.

L

ON THE FINDHORN.

She brought up a bairn there, in a hollow stone that was ance a font for holy water. I mind the laddie weel; he grew up a browe loon (Moray-shire for a 'stout boy') and was pauper at our school." "*Unfortunate,*" replied the stranger with much emotion, "but never *worthless!*" He took up his summer abode in Elgin; and some years afterwards assigned the bulk of his property to endow a hospital for ten old and indigent persons, a school of industry for sixty poor children, and a free school for two hundred and thirty scholars. The building was to be called " the Elgin Institution," the founder desiring to suppress his own name; but as "Anderson's" it is, and doubtless always will be known. A story like this gives dignity to a somewhat common-place-looking edifice, which surpasses even the time-worn splendours of the cathedral!

DULSIE BRIDGE.

The Highland railway itself leaves Strathspey near Grantown, and proceeds directly northwards, first climbing to the summit of a "blasted heath" (but not Shakspeare's) on the road to FORRES. The descent to this famous place is long. I did not find it very interesting. "*How far is't called to Forres?*" was a question that recurred irresistibly. At length I alighted,

CAWDOR CASTLE.

and soon found comfortable quarters, after a journey filled with excitement and delight. Two or three days were spent here in exploring the neighbourhood, especially the course of the Findhorn. Nothing that I had heard or read had prepared me for the exceeding beauty of this river, dashing as it does over its rocky bed, amid vast granite boulders and between high, precipitous, wooded banks; the brown water, with crests and fringes of white foam, hurrying tumultuously onward in rapid and innumerable small cataracts. There are some charming grounds, through which a path leads above the river, traversing noble woods. Soon after emerging, I came upon the junction of a mountain torrent, the Divie, with the Findhorn, and walked a little way up the lovely glen, returning, however, to the main stream, and following its course upwards as far as Dulsie Bridge—a walk altogether of some thirteen or fourteen miles from Forres, as rich in picturesque beauty as any ramble in these islands. "What spot on earth," writes Mr. St. John, "can exceed in beauty the landscape comprising the old bridge of Dulsie, spanning with its lofty arch the deep, dark pool, shut in by grey and fantastic rocks, surmounted with the greenest of greenswards, with clumps of ancient weeping birches, backed by the dark pine trees?" The bridge, as will be seen from our cut, consists of one bold lofty arch spanning the yawning chasm, and of one smaller subsidiary one, carrying the roadway from a high rock onwards to the north bank. The greater arch is 46 feet in width. Here are indications even yet of "the Morayshire Floods" in 1829, when the wild little river rose between its granite banks to a height of forty or fifty feet above its ordinary level,[1] overspreading much of the neighbouring country, sweeping away stone bridges, and spreading so much desolation around that the catastrophe has become an epoch of reckoning; and old people at Forres will tell you of events "before the Flood." At Dulsie Bridge the mass of water was so confined that it completely filled the smaller arch, and rose in the greater to within three feet of the keystone; being thus no less than forty feet in perpendicular height above the usual level. From this spot a "machine" carried me by a good road to Cawdor, where the castle again called up Shakspearean recollections. The building is a fine unmodernized specimen of feudal architecture, with drawbridge and battlemented tower, commanding a magnificent view over the surrounding country. The old and splendid trees by which it is environed increase its charm.

> "*Duncan.* This castle hath a pleasant seat; the air
> Nimbly and sweetly recommends itself
> Unto our gentle senses.
>   *Banquo.*   This guest of summer,
> The temple-haunting martlet, does approve,
> By his loved mansionry, that the heaven's breath
> Smells wooingly here : no jutty, frieze,
> Buttress, nor coign of vantage, but this bird
> Hath made his pendent bed, and procreant cradle :
> Where they most breed and haunt, I have observed,
> The air is delicate." [2]

From Cawdor, a pleasant drive of six miles along the broad valley of the Nairn, leads to the town at the mouth of the river, also called Nairn, with

[1] See *The Morayshire Floods*, by Sir T. D. Lauder, Bart.
[2] Shakspeare, *Macbeth*, Act i., sc. 6.

its broad grassy and sandy beach, unsurpassed, I should think, for bathing purposes. This also was a place that invited a longer stay, from the clear freshness of its air, as well as for the charms of the beautiful Moray Firth, with the distant view of Ben Wyvis rising grandly to the west, beyond the Black Isle and the head of Cromarty Firth. But time pressed, and I had to return to the little inn at Forres by rail. It would have been easy to reach Inverness from Nairn, passing near Culloden Moor, where Prince Charles was defeated in 1746 by the Duke of Cumberland, and the cause of the Stuarts was finally lost. The battle-field, on the moor of Drummossie, is three miles from the Culloden station : a bleak and melancholy waste, not inappropriate to that scene of slaughter. "The ground, it will be seen, was admirably adapted for the Royalists—strong in horse and artillery, and

CULLODEN MOOR.

everything else appears, as if by a fatality, to have conduced to their success. Prince Charles was obliged to fight to protect Inverness, but he might have chosen better ground than this. He had won every battle that he had fought—he had not abused his successes by misconduct—and yet his army was demoralised as though by a succession of defeats. The pay of the men had been long in arrear, and among the officers there was jealousy and distrust of one another. The whole of the previous day the army had but one biscuit per man, and it had been marching all night with the intention of surprising the duke. This it had failed to do, and was now going to fight upon the most unsuitable ground that could have been selected. And to crown all, at the last moment arose that ever-recurring difficulty about the position on the right wing. The Macdonalds claimed it as their right from time immemorial. The Stewarts and Camerons were placed there, and the Macdonalds on the left. The armies had been about equal in numbers, but pressed by hunger and fatigue nearly one-half the rebels had straggled into Inverness, or fallen asleep on the line of march. The Duke of Cumberland drew up his forces in three lines, and began the battle with his artillery. The French gunners in Prince Charles' service feebly replied. The Highlanders waxed impatient and began to waver. Lord George Murray, seeing no time was to be lost, led forward the clans on the right, who, charging with their usual impetuosity, broke the Duke's first line. But the second, drawn up three deep, front rank kneeling, reserved their fire till the enemy were almost on their bayonet-points, and then poured in so murderous a volley as to make the Highlanders recoil. M'Lachan and M'Lean were killed, while Lochiel was carried off badly wounded. Now was the time for the Macdonalds to have proved the justice of the claim they held so tenaciously, and, like the Macphersons on a similar occasion, to have retrieved the fortunes of the day; but in vain the Duke of Perth rode up and implored them to advance. In vain Macdonald of Keppoch charged at the head of a few personal retainers, and fell, exclaiming, 'My God! do the children of my clan forsake me?' Still one chance remained, and all might yet be well. Lord Elcho galloped up to the Prince, and begged him to put himself at their head and lead the charge in person. The Prince hesitated, and declined. Lord Elcho turned away with a bitter execration, and swore he would never see his face again. A few minutes afterwards Charles suffered himself to be led from the field— the Macdonalds marched off without striking a blow, but with pipes playing and colours flying—the battle of Culloden was lost, and with it the hopes of the Stuarts." [1]

A thousand Highlanders thus gallantly laid down their lives in the last struggle for a hopeless cause; and their descendants, while admiring their courage, now unanimously admit their mistake. There are none now, as there were in the days of Sir Walter Scott, to cherish the Jacobite tradition; and though the cruelties perpetrated by the Duke of Cumberland after the battle have stamped his name with everlasting infamy, all Highland men are now loyal to the cause for which he fought.

Returning to Forres, I visited its two monuments with no little interest. The modern one, a "Pharos" in honour of Nelson, stands in a lofty position, a little to the east of the town, and commands an extensive view. "It is worth mentioning, as a fine instance of patriotic feeling, that every individual man and woman in Forres contributed by labour or money to the erection of this interesting public work." The other monument, in a field at the roadside, is the mysterious relic known as "Sweno's Stone;" a Runic obelisk, erected, says Camden, to commemorate a victory gained by King Malcolm MacKenneth over Sweno, King of Denmark. It is twenty-three feet high, and is divided into compartments, five on one side, and three on the other, all filled with rude figures of men and animals, much defaced.

---

[1] See Murray, *Guide to Scotland*, p. 369.

As far as can be made out, one set seems to represent a military triumph, while the emblems of the other point to some religious meaning: but the stone is still a puzzle to antiquaries. Some have seen in it a relic of Macbeth! The "blasted heath" where that chieftain met the witches is identified in a reach of waste land partly reclaimed, on the border of a wood, five or six miles from Forres on the road to Nairn. A spot called "Macbeth's Hill" perpetuates the tradition: but, when I passed it, the general effect of the scene was moderately cheerful, not to say common-place. There was, at any rate, no help to the imagination in the aspect of the heath, though it was possible to conjecture what it might be "in thunder, lightning, and in rain," when clouds that have gathered over the Grampians sail on the wings of the south wind, gathering blackness as they move, and at the Moray Firth seem to "mingle sea and sky."

MOUTH OF NAIRN HARBOUR IN THE FLOOD OF 1829.

THE EASTERN COAST AND DEESIDE.

CURLING.

BANKS OF THE DEVON, NEAR RUMBLING BRIDGE.

THE EASTERN COAST AND DEESIDE.

AN excursion to Scotland would hardly be complete without a visit to the Grampians from their eastern side. It is not only that some of their most characteristic beauties are thus to be seen, but that an opportunity will at the same time be given for at least a glimpse of that "Highland Home" whose name is so familiar to all the subjects of our Queen. Balmoral, Crathie, Braemar, are household words with us all, and it is as much a feeling of loyalty as a love of the picturesque that sends so many of our countrymen and countrywomen every year along that fair valley which we call Deeside. The city of ABERDEEN gives entrance to it, and may be reached most easily by a route already described, through Stirling and Perth, where a line branches eastwards to Forfar. Another way, far more interesting, is across the Firths of Forth and Tay; the traveller pausing if he will to visit DUNFERMLINE, with its singularly beautiful ruined palace wall, and the room where Charles the First was born; proceeding thence to Kinross and Loch Leven, famed for Queen Mary's romantic escape, and sparing half a day at least, to the banks of the Devon, especially to the beautiful scenery of Rumbling Bridge; and arranging, if possible for a short stay at ST. ANDREWS. This ancient city ought to be seen, if only for its fine bay and its stately ruins overlooking the sea. To another class of visitors the fine golfing links will have a supreme attraction. There is no place in Great Britain, I believe, where that fascinating game is cultivated with greater persistency and enthusiasm, or on more favourable ground. Some English readers may not precisely know what this "royal and ancient" game may be. Some have even proved so benighted as to confound it with "curling," a splendid game, also, it is true, as played over the vast smooth expanse of some frozen loch. Golf is yearly becoming more appreciated south of the border, and yet its proper home is still in the North. A few lines, therefore, from a high authority, may be quoted here.[1] "Small holes of about four inches diameter are punched in the turf at distances indefinitely variable, but ranging from about 100 to 400 or 500 yards; and from one of these holes into the next in order, a ball of guttapercha of about $1\frac{3}{4}$ ounce weight has to be driven with implements ('clubs') of some variety

LOCH LEVEN.

devised for the purpose. Their variety is determined by this, that while in starting from the hole, the ball may be 'teed' (i.e. placed where the player chooses, with a little pinch of sand under it called a 'tee') it must in every other case be played strictly from its place as it chances to be,—in sand, whin, or elsewhere,—a different club being necessary in each particular difficulty. These clubs may generally be defined as shafts of wood, with so-called 'heads' of wood or iron attached. Starting from the one hole, it is the immediate aim of the player to drive his ball as far towards the next as he

[1] *Encyclopædia Britannica*, ninth edition, vol. x. art. "Golf," by P. P. Alexander.

ROYAL PALACE, DUNFERMLINE.

can. Having got within some moderate distance of it, he proceeds to make his 'approach shot,' carefully selecting the appropriate implement. When he has reached the 'putting green,' a smooth space carefully chosen for the purpose, he essays to put (or 'putt') his ball into the hole; and generally if he does it in two strokes, he may be held skilful or fortunate. The player who 'holes' his ball in the smallest number of strokes is, as a matter of course, winner of the hole." It may be added that the circuit

ST. ANDREWS.

consists of eighteen holes, which have to be successively won. Such is the mystery of the game. The writer goes on candidly to avow that it may not seem, in this description "very lively or entertaining." "And yet," he adds, kindling with his subject into eloquence, "no game stirs a keener enthusiasm in its votaries; and very few people who have ever fairly committed themselves to the serious practice of it will be found to deny its extreme fascination. It is a manly and eminently healthful recreation, pursued as it is mostly amid the fresh sea breezes; while as exercise it has this particular merit, that, according to pace, it may be made easy or smart at pleasure, and thus equally adapts itself to the overflowing exuberance of youth, the matured and tempered strength of manhood, and the gentler decays of age."

I am bound to say that in the game, as it was my good fortune to witness it at St. Andrews, there was not much of the "exuberance of youth :" but it was interesting to see how for hours the patient middle-aged players, attended by "cadies" carrying their sheaves of clubs, followed the little balls over the sandy grassy "links," never seeming to quicken their pace, and

ST. ANDREWS CATHEDRAL : WEST FRONT.

only showing the energy that was in them when the club was uplifted for some mighty stroke, that sent the ball 180 yards or more towards its destination. The rest was science ; and the skill with which the tiny ball was sped to its resting-place was often really extraordinary. No one who has watched the game well played on these breezy uplands by the sea will wonder at its popularity. Any of us who could and would take easy healthful exercise in the finest of air, without mental distraction or excitement, for several hours together, through successive days of early summer, would find the result in the bracing and exhilaration of the whole system ; and it is into exercise like this that the game beguiles its votaries.

But we shall be accused of giving way to the tendency of the times, by thus presenting St. Andrews as famous for its golfing ground, rather than for its University. This is the oldest in Scotland, having been founded in 1411, and it has a noble record, as well as great present influence and power. New plans are proposed, as I write, for its constitution and management, and are much discussed in the Scottish newspapers. Whatever may come of these proposals, it is at any rate to be hoped that the result will be to maintain the continuity, as well as to enlarge the scope of this ancient and

PRIORY GATEWAY, ST. ANDREWS.

renowned University; the earliest of those institutions which have for centuries maintained the standard of general education in Scotland so high above that of other nations. For there has not been through all these generations a barefooted laddie in Scotland who might not hope to become a University student. The common school system instituted by John Knox, and the University system originated in St. Andrews by Bishop Wardlaw, have mainly made the Scottish people what they are; and from the latter England too has reaped the benefit, as not a few of her greatest names attest.

But when I visited St. Andrews there was no opportunity of studying even the external features of its University life. For the session was over, the college buildings seemed given up to whitewashers, masons and carpenters, and the little city was decidedly dull, save when happy bright-looking school-children streamed forth upon its pavement, reminding the spectator that St. Andrews is as famous for its elementary school system [1] as for the University itself. The time for seaside holidays had scarcely arrived, or I could have wondered at the fewness of visitors to a place which must surely be one of the most healthful and bracing resorts in Great Britain. The dry pure air was delightfully invigorating, and the view over the German Ocean in the bright summer weather, truly magnificent. Possibly a visitor's impression might have been different in other aspects of the sea and sky ; and, like our eastern shores generally, St. Andrews may be subject to the visitation of bitter east winds and driving mists, when the weather on the western coasts

THE TAY BRIDGE, PRIOR TO DECEMBER 28, 1879.

is clear and bright. Thus the balance assuredly is not entirely against the West!

From St. Andrews to Dundee, by the Tay Bridge, was but a brief run. The overthrow of that structure in the terrific storm of December 28, 1879, will be fresh in the memory of my readers. In the preceding summer I had crossed it, and, like many a passenger, had noted how frail it seemed. Yet the assurances of its safety appeared decisive, until the crisis came. A much stronger bridge will soon replace it ; meanwhile the ferry over is not un-pleasant on a calm and sunny day. Dundee itself is apt to disappoint the visitor,—very much, perhaps, because he has so often heard the city called "bonnie Dundee." Assuredly this is not exactly the epithet one would choose for the great commercial port. As the *Journal* already quoted

---

[1] Dr. Bell, the founder of the "Madras" system of instruction, was a native of St. Andrews, and the Madras College here, founded by his bequest, has about nine hundred pupils, of both sexes.

DUNDEE.

tersely puts the matter, "Dundee is a very large place, and the port is

large and open; the situation of
the town is very fine, but the town
itself is not so." No doubt the
views up and down the Tay are
imposing; but I suspect that the
"bonnie" is from the old Jacobite
songs, and means not this city at
all, but Viscount Dundee, better
known to us as John Graham of
Claverhouse! The city has at least
the interest which belongs to a
thriving centre of industry, mostly
modern, with an intelligent energetic working population; flax,
jute, and bitter oranges being con-
stantly unloaded at its busy wharves,
for the staple products of the place.
There is also a fine People's Park,
a memorial of the honoured name
of David Baxter; and from Dundee
Law, a hill in the neighbourhood,
there is a fine sea view, including

TRIUMPHAL ARCH, DUNDEE.

the Bell Rock, famed through Southey's ballad of the Abbot of Aberbrothock (Arbroath), with the lighthouse that has succeeded the "warning bell" of the old tradition.

The journey to ABERDEEN will probably not be broken, else the fine landlocked estuary of MONTROSE, should the visitor be fortunate enough to see it when the tide is high, would richly repay a few hours' tarrying, not to mention the handsome town with its breezy links, and Ferryden Craig with its magnificent view. It should be added that for travellers to Deeside who wish to leave the beaten path, there is a short cut beyond railways,

BELL ROCK LIGHTHOUSE.

through Forfarshire, by way of BRECHIN, hence twenty miles to Loch Lee, a little lake of rare beauty, surrounded by magnificent scenery, where, in farmhouse or cottage lodgings a few families spend their summer. It was a favourite retreat of the late Dr. Guthrie. Hence a road across the shoulder of Mount Keen leads to Ballater. The route is but little known; but there are few which have more to repay the lover of fine scenery who can be independent of hotels for some thirty miles of the distance. If the tourist has already seen Aberdeen, he should by all means take this journey. Otherwise he will probably prefer to visit Deeside by way of the "Granite City" and the comfortable, well-appointed railway. After Montrose, the railway runs along a level pretty country, approaching the sea near STONEHAVEN, and thence continuing near the shore with many grand glimpses of the German Ocean, until crossing the north of the Dee it enters the low-lying spacious Aberdeen station, above which tower the lofty granite houses of Castle and Union Streets. There is no more solid-looking imposing city in Great Britain. Union Street in particular is unequalled in its aspect of stately strength. But the interest of Aberdeen is chiefly in its colleges, King's and Marischal, incorporated into the University, and in its cathedral, of which the choir and transepts have been long destroyed, and only the grand nave remains. Marischal College was specially attractive for the memories of the two friends Robert

DR. GUTHRIE'S HOUSE, LOCH LEE.

Hall and James Mackintosh, who there together began their career, two lads of eighteen or nineteen. "They read together," says Hall's biographer, "they sat together at lecture, if possible; they walked together. In their joint studies, they read much of Homer and Herodotus, and more of Plato; and so well was all this known, exciting admiration in some, in others envy, that it was not unusual, as they went along, for their class-fellows to point at them and say, ' *There go Plato and Herodotus !* ' But the arena in which they met most frequently was that of morals and metaphysics, furnishing topics of incessant disputation. After having sharpened their weapons by reading, they often repaired to the spacious sands upon the sea-shore, and still more frequently to the picturesque scenery on the banks of the Don, above the old town, to discuss with eagerness the various subjects to which their attention had been directed. There was scarcely an important position in Berkeley's *Minute Philosopher*, in Butler's *Analogy*, or in Edwards *On the Will*, over which they had not thus debated with the utmost intensity. Night after night, nay, month after month, for two sessions, they met only to study or to dispute; yet no unkindly feeling ensued. The process seemed rather, like blows in that of welding iron, to knit them closer together." [1]

After visiting the noble library of King's College, I wandered to the Old Town. It lies on the way to the mouth of the river Don, and in its amplitude and repose affords a strange contrast to the great and busy city

LOCH LEE CHURCHYARD.

a mile away. The *aber*, or river mouth, of Aberdeen, it should be noted, is that of the *Don*, not of the *Dee*, as some have supposed; and so the citizens are often called "Aberdonians." Yet the tide of population and commerce has long been shifted to the latter river. A little way beyond the Old Town is the famous Bridge of Don, otherwise known as the Brig o' Balgownie, made famous by Lord Byron, who spent the first ten years of his life at Aberdeen, and to whose youthful fancy the old prediction respecting it had a strange and awful fascination—

> "Brig o' Balgownie, black's your wa';
> Wi' a wife's ae son, an' a mare's ae foal,
> Down ye shall fa'."

* *Life of Rev. R. Hall*, by Dr. Olinthus Gregory, *Hall's Works*, vol. vi. pp. 14, 15.

Byron, be it remembered, was an only son. But the bridge has not fallen yet, and its tall pointed arch has outlasted more than five centuries and a half of change.

When last at Aberdeen, I had the opportunity of attending a performance by the "Dundee Children's Choir" of Handel's *Messiah.* The choir, it appears, is composed of scholars from the different board schools; and a party of 220 of these were visiting Aberdeen for the evening, with about sixty grown-up singers for the bass and tenor parts. Three-fourths of the singers were actually children, from eight years old to fourteen, and very beautifully they sang. I never heard children's singing so sweet and true. A tall tenor, and a bass singer, who took the necessary solos, looked like good-natured giants in front of the little mites! The soprano solos were sung by children themselves, and the effect was very thrilling and tender, while the choruses were delightful. There was a very large and enthusiastic audience, and the general effect was truly impressive. Perhaps Scottish children can undertake such a task more gravely and seriously than would be the case in England: certainly there were no signs of self-consciousness or of a tendency to display: and a pleasanter evening has rarely been spent by me, than in listening to those little folks from Dundee.

The "Deeside Railway" to Ballater pursues its way through a country beautifully wooded, and for the most part close beside the river, which in a swift and lovely flood comes down from the hills. At the time of my visit the woods that lined the banks were still brown and leafless, save where fir-trees were abundant. By degrees we gained the upper levels, where the view beyond the river was grandly closed by dark hills, with streaks and fields of snow. Ballater at last was reached—a village on a somewhat considerable plain, where the river makes a great curve before fairly entering the region of the hills. A conical wooded hill, Craig-an-darroch, "crag of the oaks," rising close by the village, gives a picturesqueness to the scene, which otherwise would be somewhat tame. This hill should be ascended for the sake of the view to be obtained, at a very slight expenditure of time and trouble, of the river Dee, both upward and downward; the Grampian heights closing in the prospect to the west. To the North is Morven, bare and massive, though scarcely beautiful, and disappointing to those who have formed their anticipations from Byron's lines:

"When I roved a young Highlander o'er the dark heath,
   And climbed thy steep summit, O Morven, of snow,
   To gaze on the torrents that thundered beneath,
   Or the mist of the tempest that gathered below."

The so-called "Pass of Ballater" runs behind Craig-na-darroch, and is simply a narrow lane separating it from the heights that rise steeply beyond. It is overrated, I think, by those who call it "romantic." The true beauty of the neighbourhood is upon the open road that leads from Ballater. This was now comparatively deserted. Public conveyances had not yet begun running, and the glorious freshness of the spring air, the beauty of the sunshine, and the tender grace of the early flowers, were all lavished on a stray tourist or two, with a few elderly salmon fishers, stalwart educated gentlemen

OLD ABERDEEN.

from the south, whose evening talk, though naturally dealing over much with sport, was very pleasant. They seemed like men who had done a good work in life, and who now had a right to their enjoyment. I left them by the river-bank, while pursuing my way to Braemar. There was a little characteristic scene at starting. It appears that the post-cart, here as

LOCHNAGAR.

elsewhere, is allowed to take a few passengers. I therefore asked the driver, a youth, whether he had a place to spare. Quite imperturbably, he answered, *No !* It was a specimen of the way in which Scottish people spare their words. In the south, it would probably have been " *The places are all taken, Sir, to-day ;*" or " *Very sorry, but we are full this morning.*" But the driver's *No* was at least sufficient, and not another word did he speak. Not that he was inconsiderate, for he readily consented to take my knapsack to Braemar for the small sum of sixpence. And here again was a little incident quite as characteristic. All this took place in front of the post office. I had not wherewithal to pay the sixpence—only gold, for which the postmistress had not sufficient change, but she at once took up sixpence and handed it me, saying, "Oh I'll lend it ye, Sir !" not knowing of course whether she would ever see me again, and apparently not caring—on that ground, at least ! The walk was grand ; the beautiful Dee was with me all the way, now and then receding in lovely bends round fir-clad peninsulas, but soon reappearing. Its music was unceasing—how is it that guide books do not mention this special charm ? I suppose it is because with most travellers the noise of wheels and the clatter of conversation drown the more exquisite melody. Every mountain river, it has been said, has its own peculiar *tone,* and certainly the song of the Dee, whether in its ripple or its bolder dash, was characteristic all along. The mountains gradually swelled to greater vastness ; Lochnagar, especially (so-called from a lakelet, "The Hare's Loch," at its base), with its peaks and curves, its recesses and precipices, now white with dazzling snow, was not unworthy of the Oberland. As in Switzerland, too, the lesser heights in the foreground were covered with pine forests, interspersed with woods of birch and alder, with that lovely April flush upon their brownness that presages the breaking into leaf.

Some of Lord Byron's earliest associations were with the mountain scenery of this district, and he has recorded his impressions in lines, less artistic perhaps, but more genuine in their sentiment, than many of his later poems.

> " Away, ye gay landscapes, ye gardens of roses !
>   In you let the minions of luxury rove ;
> Restore me the rocks, where the snow-flake reposes,
>   Though still they are sacred to freedom and love :
> Yet, Caledoni,a beloved are thy mountains,
>   Round their white summits though elements war :
> Though cataracts foam 'stead of smooth flowing fountains,
>   I sigh for the valley of dark Lochnagar.
>
> Ah ! there my young footsteps in infancy wandered,
>   My cap was the bonnet, my cloak was the plaid,
> On chieftains long perished my memory pondered,
>   As daily I strode through the pine-covered glade.

> I sought not my home till the day's dying glory
>   Gave place to the rays of the bright polar star ;
> For fancy was cheered by traditional story,
>   Disclosed by the natives of dark Lochnagar."

For miles I met nobody : reaching in due course the Prince of Wales's shooting lodge Abergeldie, on the opposite side of the river. There, by the way, I noticed what I had heard before, that the banks of the river are lined with beautiful birch tree woods. The birks of *Abergeldie* being famous, Burns was led partly by the alliteration to celebrate instead the "birks of Aberfeldy," which are also fine, though far inferior in number to these beside the Dee. The tower of Balmoral next rose into view, low down amid a grand amphitheatre of hills. On a knoll to the right stood the little church of Crathie, humble and simple in appearance, very like many a village chapel in England. On the other side of the road, towards the river, is the little churchyard, surrounding the ruins of the "auld kirk," a very vale of rest amid the silence and splendours of the mountains. Her Majesty's faithful attendant Mr. John Brown had been interred there only a few days before. It was easy to discover his grave, in an inclosure where are grave-stones to his ancestors and relatives, most of them erected by himself. The grave was covered with wreaths of immortelles and other flowers : many with cards attached bearing the names of the givers ; princesses, countesses, some other great people, and John Brown's own associates and kindred. One wreath had on the card " A tribute of love to dear Uncle John from his little niece, Victoria." Probably the Queen had been godmother to his brother's or sister's child. At the head of the grave was a wreath of some lovely purple flower, with the Queen's card attached to it, and in her own handwriting the words : *A tribute of loving grateful and everlasting friendship and affection from his truest best and most faithful friend, Victoria R. and I.* It was very touching to have such an illustration before one's own eyes of that spirit of true-hearted faithful service which seems like a tradition of the past.

Balmoral itself need not be described : its outward form is familiar to us all. In beauty of situation, as beauty is reckoned in the Highlands, it is almost incomparable, being surrounded by the grandeur of forest sweep and purple mountains, and, at the time of my visit, vast dazzling snow-fields, with the blue sky and sunshine over all, and the pellucid, rushing, singing Dee beneath. In different directions the heights are surmounted by cairns, beehive-shaped, commemorative of royal visits, birthdays, and other events. These do not, perhaps, add to the impressiveness of the scenery : yet it was impossible not to sympathise with the feelings which have thus sought expression. They tell of a blithe and happy *family* life in past days, such as we do not always associate with our ideas of royalty.

The grounds of the castle appeared in perfect order, with lawns,

BALMORAL CASTLE FROM THE RIVER.

paths, and drives, all approached by a bridge, as the palace is on the opposite side of the river from the main road: but access is rigorously forbidden whether Her Majesty is there or not. All looked very lonely: not even a gardener was visible in the grounds, and the blinds of the palace windows were all down. The only sign of movement about the place was in the clock at the top of the tower, which was going as usual, and struck *one* as I was looking on, reminding me of luncheon, that soon was obtained at a charming little roadside inn at Crathie, a mile farther on, exquisitely clean and beautifully situated. In fact, so attractive was the place that I instantly engaged a lodging for a night on my return; my business was now to get to BRAEMAR, or rather, as it should be called in full, Castleton of Braemar. The walk now became surpassingly beautiful—the road leading through pine-woods that extend to the river's edge, while the endless mountain forms, black with heather, grey with granite, richly green with firs, and in the back ground ever lustrous with snow, gave a variety and charm to every turn. In many places there were fearful signs of the late winter's havoc. Vast forests had been cut through by the gale almost as cleanly as standing corn by the sweep of the sickle, and the gaps were strewn with hundreds of uprooted trees, some lifting their roots high in air, grasping huge stones and masses of earth, as if in convulsive effort to stay the catastrophe.

At length a few people appeared upon the lonely road—a very few, but sufficiently numerous to show that groups of human habitations could not be far off. Then Castle Braemar was seen, and immediately afterwards, to the left, the village of Castleton, high up on a hill slope or brae, commanding, of course, an extensive view of valleys and mountains. In a comfortable hotel the only other occupant was again a salmon-fisher, disappointed but aspiring. "There are no fish in the Dee this year," he said, "there is no sport at all!" Yet he seemed to enjoy himself so much that I could not help suggesting there was plenty of *sport*, though perhaps no *salmon* —a view of the matter which seemed to comfort him a little. However, he was off the next morning from the Dee to the Don, hoping for better results, and I was left alone to explore this fine village, and to breathe its exhilarating air—the purest, it is said, and most bracing in Great Britain, according to the ozone standard. Yet its mountains are here too near to make the scenery very grand, as for the full effect of mountain prospects a clear space is required, opening up to the loftier heights which of necessity recede from the rest. But the glory of Braemar is that in all directions paths lead directly to the mountain solitudes and sublimities; while the Dee may be followed by "linns" and rapids and a vast rocky wilderness, to the point where the infant stream leaps from a ledge a thousand feet high, and begins its swift journey to the sea. I could not penetrate to this ledge, high up among the secrets of the Cairngorm mountains; although those who have followed the path between the stupendous heights of Ben Muich Dhui to the right and Cairn Toul to the left, crossing the summit of the glen by the Pass of Larig, and descending through the Rothiemurchus forest to Aviemore, declare that there is nothing so fine in all Scotland. It was possible only to take the comparatively easy road which leads upwards to the head of Glen Tilt, commanding after the first mile or two a magnificent view across the valley of the highest mountains in the Grampian range; Ben Muich Dhui, the loftiest of all, being grandly conspicuous. Some pretty falls are passed at the Linn of Corriemulzie, and at six miles distance the Linn of Dee is reached, where a handsome bridge of white Aberdeen granite, opened by the Queen in September 1857, spans the river. The Linn itself is a narrow fissure between slaty rocks, through which the river chafes and tumbles; and at the time of my visit, the melting snows having swollen the torrent almost to the projecting edges of the rocks, the force of the river was tremendous. Three miles beyond this the river-side is left, and the climb to the water-shed fairly commences. But to attempt this the snow forbade, and there was nothing for it but to return to Braemar, taking now the opposite, or left bank of the Dee, and visiting on the way the pretty glen and Linn of Quoich, "the Cup." Some distance below this glen the little Sluggan Water falls into the Dee, and is spanned near the juncture by one of General Wade's bridges.

The route by Glenshee past "the Spital," or *Hospice*, a good, though in parts very tedious carriage-road in summer, to Blairgowrie and the valley of the Tay, was likewise impracticable. I could only take this road for a little distance up the beautiful Glen Clunie, and my visit to Braemar was over.

The Braemar Highlands, like most far-spreading mountain regions, have many a tale and tradition of ancient strife, with weird stories of the super-natural, such as the winter terrors of the mountain land may well suggest. A long evening on my return to the charming inn at Crathie was spent in reading these tales of olden time. I was amused to find that the district had, like other mountain countries of the west and east, its William Tell. Here is the narrative.

"A young man named M'Leod had been hunting one day in the Royal Forest. A favourite hound of the king's having attacked M'Leod, was killed by him. The king soon heard of the slaughter of his favourite, and was exceedingly angry—so much so, that M'Leod was condemned to death.

"The gibbet was erected on *Craig Choinnich, i.e.* Kenneth's Craig. As there was less of justice than revenge in the sentence, little time was permitted ere it was carried into execution. The prisoner was led out by the north gate of the castle. The king, in great state, surrounded by a crowd of his nobles, followed in procession. Sorrowing crowds of the people came after, in wondering amazement. As they moved slowly on, an incident

176

SCENE IN THE GRAMPIANS : FAIR WEATHER.

SCENE IN THE GRAMPIANS : STORMY.

LINN OF DEE.

occurred which arrested universal attention. A young woman with a child in her arms came rushing through the crowd, and, throwing herself before the king, pleaded with him to spare her husband's life, though it should be at the expense of all they possessed.

"Her impassioned entreaties were met with silence. Malcolm was not to be moved from his purpose of death. Seeing that her efforts to move the king were useless, she made her way to her husband, and throwing her

181

arms round him, declared that she would not leave him—she *would* die with him.

"Malcolm was somewhat moved by the touching scene. Allen Durward, noticing the favourable moment, ventured to put in the suggestion that it was a pity to hang such a splendid archer.

"'A splendid archer, is he?' replied the king; 'then he shall have his skill tried.'

"So he ordered that M'Leod's wife and child should be placed on the opposite side of the river; something to serve as a mark was to be placed on the child's head. If M'Leod succeeded in hitting the mark, without injuring his wife or child, his life was to be spared, otherwise the sentence was to be carried into immediate execution. Accordingly (so the legend goes) the young wife and her child were put across the river, and placed on *Tom-ghainmheine;* according to some, a little farther down the river, near where a boat-house once stood. The width of the Dee was to be the distance separating M'Leod from his mark.

"He asked for a bow and *two* arrows; and having examined each with the greatest care, he took his position. The eventful moment came; the people gathered round him and stood in profound silence. On the opposite side of the river his wife stood, the central figure of a crowd of eager bystanders, tears glistening on her cheeks as she gazed alternately at her husband and child in dumb emotion.

"M'Leod took aim; but his body shook like an aspen leaf in the evening breeze. This was a trial for him far harder than death. Again he placed himself in position; but he trembled to such a degree that he could not shoot, and, turning to the king, who stood near, he said in a voice scarcely articulate in its suppressed agony, 'This is hard.'

"But the king relented not: so the third time he fell into the attitude; and as he did so, almost roared, 'This is hard!' Then, as if all his nervousness and unsteadiness had escaped through the cry, he let the arrow fly. It struck the mark. The mother seized her child, and in a transport of joy seemed to devour it with kisses; while the pent-up emotion of the crowd found vent through a loud cry of wonder and triumph, which repeated itself again and again as the echoes rolled slowly away among the neighbouring hills.

"The king now approached M'Leod, and, after confirming his pardon, inquired why he, so sure of hand and keen of sight, had asked for *two* arrows?

"'Because,' replied, M'Leod, 'had I missed the mark, or hurt my wife or child, I was determined *not to miss you.*'

"The king grew pale, and turned away as if undecided what to do. His better nature prevailed; so he again approached M'Leod, and with kindly voice and manner told him that he would receive him into his body-guard, and that he would be well provided for.

"'Never,' answered the undaunted Celt. 'After the painful proof to which you have just put my heart, I could never love you enough to serve you faithfully.'

"The king in amazement cried out, 'Thou art a Hardy! and as Hardy thou *art*, so Hardy thou *shalt* be.' From that time, M'Leod went under the appellation of Hardy, while his descendants were termed the MacHardys, Mac being the Gaelic word for son.

"'Why, that is a corruption of the story of William Tell,' I rather uncourteously remarked, on hearing for the first time this MacHardy legend.

BRIDGE OVER SLUGGAN WATER, NEAR BRAEMAR.

"The old lady who had just related it retorted with considerable warmth, and ended by asking *when* the story of William Tell took place.

"'About the year 1307,' I replied.

"'There,' she said, with such an air of triumph, "I thought that: the William Tell story happened in 1307, and ours in 1060 or thereabouts, more than 200 years before. Na, na! our story is nae a corruption of William Tell, though William Tell's may weel be a corruption of ours.'"[1]

[1] *The Braemar Highlands : their Tales, Traditions, and History*, by Elizabeth Taylor. Nimmo, 1869, pp. 99-103.

The similarity in the popular legends of mountain lands is a topic for interesting discussion. But we cannot stay to consider it here. The romance is sufficient now; the *rationale* may be left to another season.

It will be observed that many of these stories are connected with the names of families or clans, of which they assign the origin. Another tale accounts for the origin of the Stuarts. The author says that it was "noted down from an old record belonging to one of the residents." It may be older than Shakspeare, presenting one form of the tradition which he has immortalised in *Macbeth*. There is no mention, it will be seen, of King Duncan's murder in this version of the story.

"Duncan King of the Scots had two principal men whom he employed on all matters of importance—Macbeth and Banquho. They, travelling together in a wood one day, met three fairies: the first, after making her obeisance, saluted Macbeth as Thane of Glamis; the second, Thane of Cawdor; the third, King of Scotland.

"When Banquho complained loudly of their unequal dealing in giving all the honours to Macbeth, one of them thus addressed him: 'Be content, Banquho; for though you will never be King of Scotland, a race of kings will proceed from you that will rule it for ever.'

"Macbeth was scarce warm in his seat as king ere he thought of the prediction given to Banquho; and to prevent its fulfilment, caused him to be killed, and all his posterity. But by some means Fleance, one of his sons, escaped, and fled to Wales, where he prospered greatly, and was married to the prince's daughter of that court.

"Fleance had a son named Walter, who returned to Scotland in the time of Edgar, Malcolm Canmore's son. And Edgar not only restored Walter to all Banquho's estates and honours, but made him steward over all his house,—the name and office of Stewart becoming hereditary in his posterity.

"From this Walter the steward descended Robert Stewart, who succeeded David Bruce in the kingdom of Scotland. For this Robert II., surnamed Stuart, became King of Scotland by descent from the eldest sister of David Bruce, and was also extracted from the ancient princes of Wales, by Fleance, as before said; thus restoring British blood to the throne of Scotland.

"Thus the name of Stuart originated; and in early times it was one of the predominant names in Braemar."

But we must leave these old stories now, for to-morrow will take us by a long journey back to Aberdeen and Inverness; the far north is as yet unexplored, and we must have at least a glimpse of its glens, mountains, and far-away islands before bidding farewell to Scotland.

TO THE FAR NORTH.

SUNDAY ON THE NORTHERN COAST : GOING HOME.

KIRKABISTER LIGHTHOUSE.

TO THE FAR NORTH.

ST. DUTHUS' CHURCH, TAIN.

WE enter now a region beyond the usual tourist haunts, and decidedly inferior to these in its attractions to the lover of scenery. Yet all who delight most in breezy health-giving uplands, and yet more those who can secure the opportunities of sport which every glen and loch and stream in these vast solitary regions afford, will be ready to place a visit to Sutherlandshire as the crowning delight of a sojourn in Scotland. North of the "Skye Railway," whose course we have already described, lies a wide and comparatively unpeopled region, comprising part of Ross-shire, the counties of Sutherland and Caithness; with bits of Cromarty here and there, as though that shire had been wrecked by some convulsion of nature, and its fragments scattered east and west. Sutherlandshire extends from sea to sea. Already in these pages we have given some description of its western coast, with cliffs scarred and broken by the fury of the Atlantic, and innumerable lochs and bays indenting the shore. The northern coast is not dissimilar; one of its lochs, Eriboll, with its transparent waters and bare shadowing hills, being one of the most beautiful inlets along the Scottish coast. The eastern side of the great county—or principality, shall we call it?—is in all respects a contrast. The coast line is almost unbroken, and a broad belt of cultivated land between the sea and the inland heights displays all the signs of prosperous and scientific husbandry. It is along the most fertile part of this rim that the railway runs from Golspie to Helmsdale, after having skirted the northern shore of the Moray Firth from Dingwall; then diverging to TAIN, on the Firth of Dornoch, an antique, prettily-situated little town, with a church dedicated to St. Duthus, or Duthac, a bishop of Ross in the thirteenth century. It contains a finely-carved pulpit presented by the Regent Murray. From Tain the line skirts the Dornoch Firth to Bonar Bridge; then crosses to LAIRG, the headquarters of most tourists and sportsmen in Sutherlandshire. Hence roads have been carried across the wild barren country to the principal places on the western and northern coasts. One of these, as already shown, leads to the beautiful and rising western watering-place of Lochinver, passing the fishing station of Aultnagealgach, and the imposing mountain Suilven (the "Sugar Loaf"). There

"MURRAY'S PULPIT," TAIN.

is also a road by Loch Shin, "the longest and the dullest lake in Scotland," and the vast treeless Reay Deer-Forest, with a romantic descent to the pretty sea-side village of Scourie on the west; while another road less interesting leads to Tongue, on the northern coast, a wild and picturesque nook much admired by tourists, overshadowed by the magnificent peaks and precipices of Ben Loyal. These roads, it may be added, are very good and well-kept; but their solitariness is something awful, as the traveller drives mile after mile through the monotonous undulating pasture-land, among hills that can hardly be called mountains, and lochs innumerable.

It must have been a journey through scenes like these that prompted Scott's lines, introducing the Fourth Canto of the *Lord of the Isles:*

> "Stranger! if e'er thine ardent step hath traced
>   The northern realms of ancient Caledon,
> Where the proud Queen of Wilderness hath placed,
>   By lake and cataract, her lonely throne;
> Sublime but sad delight thy soul hath known,
>   Gazing on pathless glen and mountain high,
> Listing where from the cliffs the torrents thrown
>   Mingle their echoes with the eagle's cry,
> And with the sounding lake, and with the moaning sky.
>
> Yes! 'twas sublime, but sad.—The loneliness
>   Loaded thine heart, the desert tired thine eye;
> And strange and awful fears began to press
>   Thy bosom with a sad solemnity.
> Then hast thou wished some woodman's cottage nigh,
>   Something that showed of life, though low and mean;
> Glad sight, its curling wreath of smoke to spy,
>   Glad sound, its cock's blithe carol would have been,
> Or children whooping wild beneath the willows green.
>
> Such are the scenes, where savage grandeur wakes
>   An awful thrill that softens into sighs;
> Such feelings rouse them by dim Rannochs' lakes,
>   In dark Glencoe such gloomy raptures rise.
> Or further, where, beneath the northern skies,
>   Chides wild Loch Eriboll his caverns hoar—
> But, be the minstrel judge—they yield the prize,
>   Of desert dignity to that dread shore,
> That sees grim Coolin rise, and hears Coriskin roar."

The region was more populous once; and whether it was or was not a kindness to remove a peasantry who could never keep themselves much above starvation-point in this wild country, to the fertile western coast, turning the bulk of Sutherlandshire into sheep-walks and deer-forests, is one of those questions on which the wisest and most humane may well hesitate. "What has been, in fact," writes Lord Ronald Gower, "the result of the policy pursued by my grandfather in Sutherland? An increase of population, as well as of rental and wealth. Lord Stafford has been accused of causing these evictions to take place, in order to gain by them: but, as a matter of fact, between the years 1811 and 1833, not a sixpence of rent was drawn from the country; but over sixty thousand pounds were spent in improving it. If any harshness was used during the evictions, Lord Stafford cannot fairly be blamed, but the agent employed. However, it was never proved that such had been the case." [1]

Lairg is the great rendezvous; the village is on a heathery upland two miles from the station, and is not to be commended for a sojourn. But the

SUILVEN-ASSYNT, NEAR LOCHINVER.

scene both there and at the station is at times very lively; the trains in summer both ways calling three times a day, "machines" of all kinds being in readiness to carry off tourists and sportsmen to their favourite resorts, and mail-coaches, such as they are, plying three or four times a week. It is true that the visitors are comparatively few, but not even Oban finds such enthusiastic admirers; and those who have either "used up" or learned to disdain the more ordinary routes, feel when reaching this breezy hamlet that the delights of their Scottish tour are now about to begin.

[1] *Reminiscences*, vol. i. p. 85.

But we cannot now pursue our way inland. Our route lies again to the eastern coast, to Golspie, whence, as in duty bound, we visit the capital of Sutherlandshire, the old cathedral city of DORNOCH, opposite to Tain, across the Firth. "This," says Chambers, "is without exception the most miserable of all our royal burghs." Mr. Baddeley observes that it "is the smallest by several hundred inhabitants of that trio of pigmy capitals, Cromarty, Inveraray,[1] and itself." Every description of the town, the same writer adds, should begin *Once upon a time.* There may probably be now between six and seven hundred inhabitants. GOLSPIE has become the more

BEN STACK, NEAR SCOURIE.

populous and important place, partly from its nearness to Dunrobin Castle (*Dun-Robin*, "Robert's Fortress," having been built in the thirteenth century by Robert, the second Earl of Sutherland). This is the chief residence of "the Duke," of whose personality, in Sutherlandshire at least, no further

[1] But let no one despise Inveraray! There is to my mind hardly a more beautiful excursion in Scotland than one that may be taken from Dunoon on the Clyde, by the wild and beautiful Loch Eck, to Strachur on Loch Fyne, whence the traveller may reach Inveraray by ferry, with the mountains at the head of the loch rising grandly to the right, and in front the town with its castle (of the Duke of Argyll), the wooded hill of Dunaquoich rising beyond, and farther still, the vast shadowy mass of Ben Cruachan. No: Dornoch has little in common with Inveraray but its smallness.

description is necessary. As shown in our cut, the building is a modern one, the late Sir Charles Barry having reconstructed the whole. "From the terraces and steps leading down to the gardens, there are beautiful views over Moray Firth to the blue hills of Banffshire and Morayshire beyond. The garden itself is divided into parterres, and is sheltered seawards by thick belts of evergreens; but trees of the finest description flourish within a stone's throw of the shore without any protection. Unless it be at Mount

DUNROBIN CASTLE.

Edgecumbe, we can call to mind no place in Great Britain where the sea air seems to affect the timber so little." To many visitors the place will be additionally interesting from its association with the memory of the Duchess of Sutherland, so well known in the early part of our Queen's reign as the friend and promoter of every good and philanthropic cause.[1]

At Helmsdale the railway diverges once more inland, up a long glen;

[1] See the *Reminiscences* of Lord Ronald Gower for an artless picture, drawn by a manly filial hand, of a noble and beautiful life.

a fair road, however, keeps to the line of the coast, and soon enters Caith-
ness-shire over a bold, bleak, immense rocky table-land, or promontory,
called the Ord of Caithness, a tremendous barrier between the two counties,
after descending which, up to the little seaport of Wick, the inland views
become quite changed in character. With the exception of one low range
of hills, marked by three separate unpicturesque rounded peaks, the whole
country is flat, treeless, and for the most part barren, peaty, with patches of
cultivation here and there, and lines of brighter verdure marking the course
of the little rivers. At Wick we meet the railway again; but unless we are

BADGALL BAY, EDRACHILLIS; ON THE WESTERN COAST.

enthusiastic anglers there is little or nothing to attract us in the route to
Halkirk and THURSO. The last named town, however, is finely situated on
a wide bay, and, after the little villages and the scanty population with
which we have lately become familiar, is somewhat surprising from its size and
substantial appearance. The piles of paving-stones in the yards and on the
wharf will attract every visitor's notice. They belong to the old "Devonian"
red sandstone, and are sent all over the kingdom. Many visitors will recal
the name of Robert Dick, the baker of Thurso, who amid the greatest
privations attained to a mastery of geological and botanical science, which

has placed his name among the highest in the rank of self-taught men. There is a handsome obelisk in the cemetery, to his memory.

But it is to "John o' Groat's House" that the curious traveller will desire to wend his way. This extreme northerly point of Scotland may be reached by road, either from Wick along the eastern coast or from Thurso along the north. The ruins of the famous House are still to be seen, and there is now a comfortable inn, commanding a fine view over the Pentland Firth, and embracing the Orkney Isles. Who knows not the legend? Yet we may tell it again for old association's sake. The family of Groat, it is said, was of Dutch descent; Groat, or Groot, being the same name as

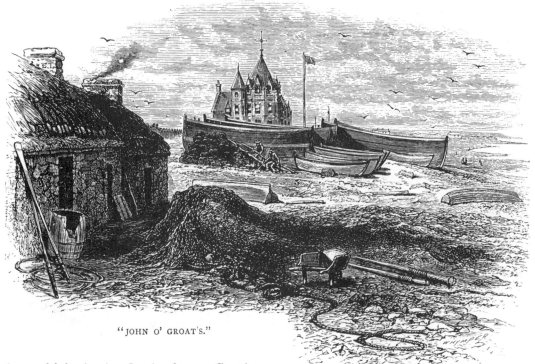

"JOHN O' GROAT'S."

that which in its Latin form, *Grotius*, is so famous. The founder of the Scottish branch of this family was, however, a Lowlander, who in the reign of James the Fourth settled in this northern region. His descendants became numerous, and eight several heads of househoulds were accustomed to assemble once a year to celebrate the memory of their ancestor. A dispute arose concerning precedency, each claiming to be head of the feast. The quarrel became inveterate, and the clan of Groat seemed in danger of being dissolved by intestine feuds; when one of them whose name was John, proprietor of the ferry to Orkney, erected during a year which intervened between two of their meetings an octagonal building with a door and window on every side, and a table in the interior to correspond, inviting each kinsman when the festal day arrived to enter by his separate door and to take his seat accordingly. The ingenuity and humour of this plan removed all scruples, and all being equally placed the struggle for primacy was forgotten. The story may be true or not: it is certainly very much akin to that of King Arthur and his Round Table. It was probably a parable, to begin with, and thus became a myth: but, whether history or legend, it has a meaning worth consideration still!

We have now reached the northern apex, the peak of the conical cap, if the comparison be not too irreverent, by which Scotland is crowned. In one of those quaint pleasant little essays which used to form a distinguishing feature

SMOO CAVE, NEAR DURNESS; ON THE NORTHERN COAST.

of *Chambers's Journal*, one of the brothers, I think it was Robert, started the idea that the form of the country was that of an *old woman*, in the position usually attributed to witches, Banffshire and Aberdeenshire being the hump, and the western coast of Sutherland being the wrinkled front. Paint Caithness red, as in some coloured maps, and the witch-picture is complete without " making believe very much." Yes, the witchery is real, only of another kind!

And beyond the point of coast where, above John o' Groat's, Duncansbay Head with its precipices and chasms fronts the northern sea, still new wonders lie. First, the Pentland Frith, with its tumultuous agitated waters, then the ORKNEYS, with their endless convolutions of cliff and coast, their thirty inhabited islands and their almost innumerable rocks and islets, attract, but do not long detain the traveller. The best view is from the outside, and from the west. The little towns of Kirkwall and Stromness may be visited; both on the island which is called Mainland, or (inappropriately enough) Pomona—the latter town being especially interesting, as having given occasion by its geological phenomena for one of Hugh Miller's most brilliant essays against the doctrine of Evolution, as propounded in the once famous *Vestiges of the Natural History of Creation*. For there was a theory of evolution before Mr. Darwin, and the great Cromarty stone-mason addressed himself to its refutation with a fulness of information, a power and brilliancy of argument which few since his time have rivalled. The Asterolepis (star-scale) of Stromness, in his hands, became a sign of Divine

AULTNA ;EALGACH, SUTHERLANDSHIRE.

creative power; and notwithstanding all the advance in knowledge which has been made since his day, the discussion may still be read with conviction as well as with admiration. The argument is briefly that the very oldest vertebrate remains are complete in organization: whereas, had the species been developed from a lower type, there must have been intermediate links discoverable. The argument has been repeatedly urged in various forms: and it has never been answered, save by the conjecture that somewhere and somehow the "missing links" may come to light. But every fresh series of observations reduces the value of this hypothesis. It is inconceivable that if the stages of transition were in truth discoverable they should not have been discovered ere now. There is no more eloquent or convincing passage in Hugh Miller's work than that in which he applies this argument to the presumed transmutation of the algæ to land-plants; [1] and the same considerations, when applied to the vaster processes required by the later form of the development theory, are even more cogent. It may not be out of place to quote a paragraph or two, as not yet out of date:

"Along the green edge of the Lake of Stennis, selvaged by the line of detached weeds with which a recent gale had strewed its shores, I marked that for the first few miles the accumulation consisted of marine algæ, here and there mixed with tufts of stunted reeds or rushes, and that

STACK POLLY, FROM LOCH LURGAN, COIGACH, WEST SUTHERLAND.

as I receded from the sea it was the algæ that became stunted and dwarfish, and that the reeds, aquatic grasses, and rushes, grown greatly more bulky in the mass, were also more fully developed individually, till at length the marine vegetation altogether disappeared, and the vegetable debris of the shore became purely lacustrine,—I asked myself whether here, if anywhere, a transition flora between lake and sea ought not to be found? For many thousand years ere the tall gray obelisks of Stennis, whose forms I saw this morning reflected in the water, had been torn from the quarry,

[1] See *Footprints of the Creator*, pp. 240-256.

or laid down in mystic circle on their flat promotories, had this lake admitted the waters of the sea, and been salt in its lower reaches and fresh in its higher. And during this protracted period had its quiet, well-sheltered bottom been exposed to no disturbing influences through which the delicate process of transmutation could have been marred or arrested. Here, then, if in any circumstances, ought we to have had, in the broad permanently brackish reaches, at least indications of a vegetation intermediate in its nature between the monocotyledons of the lake and the algæ of the sea; and yet not a vestige of such an intermediate vegetation could I find among the up-piled debris of the mixed floras, marine and lacustrine. The lake possesses no such intermediate vegetation. As the water freshens in its middle reaches, the algæ become dwarfish and ill-developed; one species after another ceases to appear, as the habitat becomes wholly unfavourable to it; until at length we find, instead of the brown, rootless, flowerless fucoids and confervæ of the ocean, the green, rooted, flower-bearing flags, rushes, and aquatic grasses of the fresh water. Many thousands of years have failed to originate a single intermediate plant. And such, tested by a singularly extensive experience, is the general evidence. There is scarce a chain-length of the shores of Britain and Ireland that has not been a hundred and a hundred times explored by the botanist,—keen to collect and prompt to register every rarity of the vegetable kingdom; but has he ever yet succeeded in transferring to his herbarium a single plant caught in the transition state?

"It will not do to tell us,—as Cuvier was told, when he appealed to the fact, determined by the mummy birds and reptiles of Egypt, of the fixity of species in all, even the slightest particulars, for at least three thousand years,—that immensely extended periods of time are necessary to effect specific changes, and that human observation has not been spread over a period sufficiently ample to furnish the required data regarding them.

"It is *not true* that human observation has not been spread over a period sufficiently extended to furnish the necessary data for testing the development hypothesis. In one special walk,—that which bears on the supposed transmutation of algæ into terrestrial plants,—human observation *has* been spread over what is strictly analogous to *millions* of years. For extent of space in this matter is exactly correspondent with duration of time. No man, in this late period of the world's history, attains to the age of five hundred years; and as some of our larger English oaks have been known to increase in bulk of trunk and extent of bough for five centuries together, no man can possibly have seen the same huge oak pass, according to Cowper, through its various stages of 'treeship,'—

'First a seedling hid in grass;
  Then twig; then sapling; and, as century rolls
  Slow after century, a giant bulk,
Of girth enormous, with moss-cushioned root
Upheaved above the soil, and sides embossed
With prominent wens globose.'

But though no man lives throughout five hundred years of time, he can trace, by passing in some of the English forests through five hundred yards of space, the history of the oak in all its stages of growth, as correctly as if he *did* live throughout the five hundred years. Oaks, in the space of a few hundred yards, may be seen in every stage of growth, from the newly burst acorn, that presents to the light its two fleshy lobes, with the first tender rudiments of a leaflet between, up to the giant of the forest, in the hollow of whose trunk the red deer may shelter, and find ample room for the broad spread of his antlers. The fact of the development of the oak, from the minute two-lobed seedling of a week's growth up to the gigantic tree of five centuries, is as capable of being demonstrated by observation spread over five hundred yards of space, as by observation spread over five hundred years of time. And be it remembered, that the sea-coasts of the world are several hundred thousand miles in extent. Europe is by far the smallest of the earth's four large divisions, and it is bounded, in proportion to its size, by a greater extent of land than any of the others. And yet the sea-coasts of Europe alone, including those of its islands, exceed twenty-five thousand miles. We have results before us, in this extent of space, identical with those of many hundred thousand years of time; and if terrestrial plants were as certainly developments of the low plants of the sea as the huge oak is a development of the immature seedling just sprung from the acorn, so vast a stretch of sea-coast could not fail to present us with the intermediate vegetation in all its stages. But the sea-coasts fail to exhibit even a vestige of the intermediate vegetation. Experience spread over an extent of space analogous to millions of years of time, does not furnish, in this department, a single fact corroborative of the development theory, but, on the contrary, many hundreds of facts that bear directly against it." [1]

Yet the wonder of the Orkneys is not in its bold cliffs with their fossils, nor in the cultivated plots which cover its uplands, nor in its remarkable and mysterious sepulchral monuments and " Picts' houses," [2] nor even in the superb climate, as soft and equable as that of the Channel Islands, so much as in the

[1] *Footprints of the Creator ; or, the Asterolepis of Stromness,* by Hugh Miller, 1849, pp. 240–256.

[2] " Peculiar to the north of Scotland, beyond the Great Glen, or line of the Caledonian Canal, are certain round towers, called burghs or brocks, or Picts' castles, of unknown age and origin. The most perfect type is the tower of Mousa, on an islet in Shetland. From this example, and others less perfect, they appear to be cylinders of masonry tapering upwards into a truncated cone, or waisted like a dice-box. The walls are composed of an outer and inner concentric shell of untrimmed stones—evenly set, but without mortar. This rude masonry is bound together by four or five courses of slabs of slate placed crosswise, so as to leave in the thickness of the wall a gallery or inclined plane winding up to the top like a corkscrew, and lighted by small openings or slits in the inside. The rest of the wall is filled up with loose stones, and it may measure in thickness from ten to fifteen feet. The towers vary in height from twenty-five to forty feet, and in diameter from thirty to fifty. They were not roofed, but the inner slits open into a circular court. A low door on the ground level led into this and communicated with the winding galleries or cells, which in some instances are so low and narrow (three feet) that it is difficult to understand how any but a race of pigmies could have traversed them. Sir Walter Scott compares the tower of Mousa to a ruined pigeon-house. More than four hundred examples are known of these towers in the North and North-west of Scotland and in the Isles, for the most part more or less ruined. They are thus distributed—in Shetland, seventy-five ; Orkney, seventy ; Caithness, seventy-nine ; Sutherland, sixty ; Long Island, thirty-eight ; Skye, thirty, etc."—*Murray,* Section vi. 3.

lingering beauty of its summer days. The evening twilight magically melts into the rose-light of the dawn; night is practically unknown; you can read at midnight not only the inscriptions over the shop-doors, but the pages of a printed book. Only a little farther north, and you would see the midnight sun. No doubt there is a corresponding loss of daylight in winter, but the natives tell you that the starry nights are glorious, and there are no Arctic chills to impair the enjoyment. Few love their country better, or with better reason than the industrious, simple-minded Orcadians.

A sail of twelve hours over an often stormy sea takes the traveller from Kirkwall, the capital of the Orkneys to Lerwick, the capital of the SHETLANDS. Half-way he passes Fair Isle, an island twenty-five miles from

LOCH SHEANASKAIG, WEST SUTHERLANDSHIRE.

any other land, containing just 214 inhabitants, and causing much wonder to many who view it from without, or scramble over its craggy landing, as to the origin of its name. "Fair," it certainly is not, in the sense in which we usually understand that term of an island. We think of coral caves, of yellow sands, of grassy slopes, of groves and shady bowers. But nothing of this kind meets us here. Wild precipices are chafed by an angry sea, the access is by clefts in the rock, leading by rough steep paths to the barren summit; and perhaps the explanation is that "Fair" is not an epithet at all, but a corruption of Norwegian *Faar*, "a sheep." "Sheep island." "The Faroe Islands have the same etymology."[1] On this island one of

[1] See *The Orkneys and Shetland*, by John R. Tudor (London, 1883), pp. 430-432.

FAIR ISLE; THE "SHEEP CRAIG."

the vessels of the Spanish Armada, driven northwards, was wrecked; and the crew are said by tradition to have taught the women the art of knitting the brilliantly variegated hosiery that we call *Shetland*. The account is probably correct, as the patterns in many of these shawls are remarkably similar to those which are wrought by the Moors of Spain.[1]

But Lerwick also, the Shetland town, is famous for its knitting; the scanty pastures having long sustained a fine breed of sheep. The Shetland ponies too are famous; though these no longer roam at large. The breed is carefully maintained, not so much for their beauty as for their utility—alas! in the coal mines of England; it being found that these hardy little creatures can best endure the fatigue of continued monotonous work in those sunless depths. They accordingly are imported southward in great numbers, never to see the light of day from the time of their descent. It is a comfort to know that they are generally well cared for, and greatly petted by the miners. Often one will be rescued by some purchaser, wishing to please his children, and will spend its days in fresh air and sunlight—a happier lot, and to outward seeming more congenial. It is to be hoped that the patient little sturdy four-footed toilers in the mine know not what they lose!

The Shetland Islands contain more than 30,000 inhabitants, a hardy race, who mostly live by fishing. The number of islands is said to

FAIR ISLE; "SHALDI CLIFF."

[1] See *The Orkneys and Shetlands*, by J. R. Tudor, p. 439.

be exactly a hundred, only between thirty and forty being inhabited. Some of these are very bold in outline. The cliffs of Bressay are extraordinary: but perhaps the greatest wonder is the Holm of Noss, detached from the island of that name by a fissure between the cliffs from four to five hundred feet in depth. "The Holm consists of a rock with perpendicular sides 160 feet in height, and having a level top, the area of which is 500 feet by 170 feet. Somewhere in the seventeenth century this, apparently, inaccessible stack was scaled by a fowler for the promised reward of a cow.

LERWICK.

Once on the summit he drove in a couple of stout stakes, to which were fastened strong guy-ropes, that had been dragged over the intervening chasm, 60 feet broad, by means of a stone and a string. On these guy-ropes was fastened an oblong box, which slid easily enough down from the Noss side, where the cliff was slightly higher, to the Holm, and was hauled back on the return journey. Tradition says that the original scaler of the Holm refused to avail himself of the box, but essayed to return as he came, and, in so doing, was killed. Latterly the box was made large enough to hold a man and a sheep, and in this manner twelve sheep were taken on to and off the Holm every summer. Some few years back, however, the whole apparatus was dismantled for fear of accidents, and the summit of the Holm handed back to its original tenants, the gulls, who during the breeding season leave very little of it unoccupied."

"GIANT'S LEG," NOSS.

The climate of these islands lacks the delicious softness of the Orkneys; the constant dampness being chilly and oppressive to the visitor; although in the latest and best accounts of these northern islands we read that "Shetland, if liable to greater rainfall, has, so far as the writer can judge, a more bracing and exhilarating atmosphere during the summer months than the southern group, where at times the heat is apparently much more intense and oppressive, and in Shetland, even in the height of summer, it is always well to be provided with warm garments." [1] The inhabitants appear a

THE HOLM OF NOSS.

hardy race, honest, shrewd, and sensible. They seem peculiarly open also to the lessons and influences of Christianity, and, beside the Presbyterian churches, there is also a mission of the Baptists, which has effected great

[1] *The Orkneys and Shetlands*, by J. R. Tudor, p. 411.

good. In courtesy and intelligence the people compare favourably with those of any place in Great Britain.

It is in these islands of the North that Sir Walter Scott found much of the material for his *Pirate;* Sumburgh Head, where much of the action of the story lies, being the most southerly point of the Shetland group—a grand, bare cliff, about 300 feet in height—while the Roost of Sumburgh ("röst," Icelandic for the current or whirlpool caused by the meeting of tides) still rushes with the fury depicted by the great novelist. Some of his descriptions may even seem exaggerated, and in these times of com-

HANDA ISLAND: ABOVE SCOURIE BAY, SUTHERLANDSHIRE.

parative civilisation the counterpart may not often be found of his more strongly-marked characters. Yet on the whole the outline is wonderfully correct, as well as vivid; and the finest creation in his story, Norna of the Fitful Head, seems to have been in part a transcript from life. The grandeurs and terrors of those storm-beaten shores, with their loneliness, and the mystery beyond, quicken the sense of the supernatural, although in our own day this rather appears in the simple intense piety of a well-instructed people, than in any tendency to credulity and superstition. The inhabitants of mountain regions, it is said, have often little sense of the majesty and glory that surround them on their daily path; not so the dwellers by those wild and stormy seas. To them the lessons of the "great deep" are not wholly in vain. "The sea is His;" and "HE MADE IT," finds a response,—often confused and inarticulate, it may be,—in the hearts of men with whose whole life sublimity and terror are so closely intertwined. It was with a strange thrill of sympathy as well as awe that in a little assembly of those northern sailors and fishermen we read the old words:

"They that go down to the sea in ships,
  That do business in great waters:
These see the works of the LORD,
  And His wonders in the deep;
For He commandeth, and raiseth the stormy wind,
  Which lifteth up the waves thereof.
They mount up to the heaven, they go down again to the depths;
  Their soul is melted because of trouble.
They reel to and fro, and stagger like a drunken man,
  And are at their wit's end.
Then they cry unto the LORD in their trouble,
  And He bringeth them out of their distresses.
He maketh the storm a calm,
  So that the waves thereof are still.
Then are they glad because they be quiet.
  So He bringeth them unto their desired haven."

THE LINN OF QUOICH, BRAEMAR.

INDEX.